The Definitive Guide to Libertarian Voluntaryism

Jack Lloyd

ISBN: 9798408569052

Thank you to everyone who challenged me in my thinking and helped refine my ideas in my own journey from statist to Libertarian Voluntaryist. The many hours of online debate, conversations, and lectures were invaluable in helping coalesce my knowledge into this work.

A special "thank you" to The Pholosopher for being my best friend, helper, and inspiration, and to my Mom, Dad, and brother Josiah, who always believed in me and supported me through it all.

CONTENTS

ACKNOWLEDGMENTS

The number of people whose works have influenced my own are multitudinous and I apologize in advance for those who I may have missed in this list. I would not have the insight I do without the writings of Carl Menger, Frédéric Bastiat, John Locke, Auberon Herbert, Lysander Spooner, Ludwig von Mises, Murray N. Rothbard, Tom Woods, John Hasnas, Robert Higgs, Hans Hermann-Hoppe, Milton Friedman, David D. Friedman, Ryan Griggs, Larken Rose, Thomas Sowell, Marc Stevens, Stefan Molyneux, Ron Paul, Zander Mars, Igor Teixeira, Walter Block, and countless others who took a stand for liberty when few would.

1

WHAT IS LIBERTARIAN VOLUNTARYISM?

Libertarian Voluntaryism. It's a mouthful to say, but the words describe so much more than I can even fit into this book. At the core, it's the amalgamation between two fields of intellectual thought: property rights theory and consent ethics theory. This book attempts to bring about a robust unification of the two fields in a manner that has never been done before. In doing so, new standards and definitions are being cemented down to help give a concrete understanding of what it means to be a principled libertarian. My hope is that, once you've understood the meanings as defined here, you'll be equipped with the knowledge required to both put the principles into action and share them with others in a readily understood manner. So first, let's break down each word.

Libertarianism. Libertarianism, as used here, is the idea that property rights are a critical mechanism for establishing ethical boundaries as among humans. **Property rights** is a human psychology where people view certain scarce physical resources as being rightfully controlled by discreet human beings labelled as "owners." Owners have the ultimate right of discretion over how property may be used subject to not physically infringing on the physical property of others. How some self-described libertarians arrive at property rights may vary, but this book seeks to set a universal approach based on the empirical ways people treat each other. The philosophical principles underpinning property rights theory will be laid out in the next chapter titled, "Philosophical Foundations." For now, just know that libertarian property rights theory begins with self-ownership, the idea that each person has the highest right of claim to their own body, and that certain physical property rights in things outside the body can also be manifested and respected.

Voluntaryism. Voluntaryism is the idea that human beings should work to maximize consent and minimize the initiation of force as among humans. Force, as used here, means touching, striking, or otherwise physically invading the body or property of another. To achieve this end, Libertarian Voluntaryists seek to understand how consent is manifested, socially and scientifically, and they attempt to respect consent as best as possible given human limitations of consciousness. This principle of thought is coined as the "non-aggression principle" or N.A.P. for short. What defines "consent" and its manifestation will be laid out in the "Philosophical Foundations" chapter. For now, just know that Voluntaryism is the vehicle for how ethical human interactions are defined through consent.

When Libertarian property rights theory and Voluntaryist ethics theory combine, we arrive at a complete philosophy for how people can treat each other peaceably while reducing conflict over scarce physical resources.

Let's dive into the foundations now to see how we get there.

2

THE PHILOSOPHICAL FOUNDATIONS

The philosophical foundations require us to get deep into the nature of existence, self, and personhood. The good news is that, no matter what belief system you may be arriving from, the foundations to Libertarian Voluntaryism are so intellectually solid and empathetically relatable that you will find yourself at peace with the process. So, let's start at the beginning:

Your existence.

No matter what worldview and preconceptions you may have, whether you're a theist, atheist, spiritualist, or agnostic, your very nature of engaging with others is a performance that assumes you exist. While some may try to suggest that we are in a simulation like something out of The Matrix movie, every single person, performatively, acts as if they exist and their actions matter. To prove this to yourself, think about your interactions with other people. The act of your talking to others is itself the performance that you think that:

1.) You exist to be talking.

2.) The other person exists to be talked to.

3.) Your words matter as you attempt to relate to another person.

No amount of intellectual weaseling can cause a person to escape the performance of people acting as if they are real, that is, they exist in physical form, and should be listened to, in other words, socially engaged with. The person who attempts to convince you that we are not real is themselves performatively contradicting their words by virtue of attempting to convince you of their position. The act of argument demonstrates that the proponent believes they are real enough to be listened to and that your beliefs matter. Otherwise, why even bother arguing in the first place if nothing is real and nothing matters? Only the ramblings of a madman, a person who continually says one thing but who, in performance, continually contradicts themselves, can promote nihilism while begging for your attention and credence.

The fact that you are reading this book right now is also itself a demonstration that you value understanding the world and wish to know more about it so you can engage with it. With this in mind, we can at least settle on the idea that, even if we were theoretically in some kind of simulation or had some other kind of projected conscious state, we do not act that way purely. Human beings act as if reality, other people, and their conscious beliefs, matter.

If you're still not convinced of this default desire to act in fixed reality, think on this other hypothetical: Imagine some random stranger came up to you and told you to jump off of a 300-foot-tall building because, in doing so, you would both survive and become wealthy. Would you do so just because a random stranger told you so? What if that stranger instead asked you to do the same, but this time, it was because a magical, invisible unicorn told them to tell you to jump? Still not convinced? Well, what if that same random person instead told you to jump because God told them to? Even the most devout Christian, Jew, or Muslim would be hard-pressed to believe that jumping off a building, as instructed by a random stranger claiming God's command, would be wise.

Why is that?

The reason why is that we as human beings, no matter how spiritual or devoted to a metaphysical belief set we could be, still rely on empirical reality through our senses to make judgements about what we think is possible. Most people readily understand that gravity exists and that, if someone jumps off a building, gravity will take its toll and the earth will pull them down to a painful splattering on the pavement. We know this to be true because we can see it take place on a smaller scale with dropping a dish, jumping off stairs, and the like. You may have even seen more tragic falls take place in online videos or on the news. We know that jumping off a building is dangerous to us and, even if a random stranger appears really convinced of the fact that we will survive and magically become wealthy, we would not readily believe them about the outcome.

So, what would convince people more likely that this random stranger is correct?

Physical corroboration.

If we were to watch others jump off the building, land safely, and suddenly have money appear in their wallet, it might be more convincing that it is possible for us to do the same. If someone you knew and liked well jumped, and they survived, the plausibility would increase due to your trust in that person and your belief in their existence. If you watched multiple close friends and family members jump off, survive, and suddenly have money appear in their wallets and purses, that might even be enough to convince you to try it yourself. Of course, all of what you witnessed could very well be a trickery played on the eyes. It could be an illusion. A hologram. A false memory implanted through some futuristic mind-control device. But, no matter what it ultimately was, the experience of seeing, touching, and corroborating in empirical reality is what strengthened the belief about what was being witnessed.

All this conjectural thought process is to say that we as human beings ultimately rely on two core components for determining truth, that is, ultimate reality:

1.) Our senses.

2.) Our corroboration of experience with other human beings.

And it's not possible, as far as we can tell, to escape these limitations of human consciousness. For example, someone who takes DMT and says they see space elves in some other dimension has no means of proving that what they are witnessing is not something outside of their own mind. They can communicate what they have seen to others while on their psychedelic trip, but they are limited by their own consciousness' expression through the body in determining what that experience was, whether it was some type of astral projection to another realm, or whether it was just neural networks in their own brain firing off and creating a feeling of an out-of-body experience. Even if others also experienced the same things while taking the substance at the same time, it would only communicate that the substance produced the experience, not what the experience was in terms of what happened to consciousness. The group of people would be relegated to sharing their experiences with each other, hoping to confirm with each other that what each person saw was, indeed, a shared, real, experience. Those taking DMT could only communicate using words and artful impressions to outsiders in hopes of getting others to envision what they saw. And, even with the shared expressions, it could not be certain that others saw exactly what transpired in perfect parallel, unlike what can be replicated and viewed with recordings of the visible light-spectrum using cameras.

We face the conundrum of having to determine whether our consciousness can see ultimate truth and reality clearly.

How do people attempt this now?

Shared experience.

For example, people relate their various experiences to each other for confirmation of what they saw. It could be as simple as sharing that some food joint has spectacular-tasting tacos, or as complex as two people attempting to agree that they felt their God speak to them. No matter what level of expression, human beings are in a constant state of confirmation with each other, attempting to make sense of the world and checking their own perceptions to gauge if other people see, hear, smell, taste, and touch in the same manner as themselves.

To a degree, what is considered "madness" is often a labelled product of common consciousness, that is, what lies outside of common experience. If 20 Ph.D.-holding psychologists see a fire truck, but a homeless man looks at the same region and claims to see a giant duck, he may be considered "mad" even if the 20 Ph.D.'s groupthink is somehow wrong due to an optical illusion.

As Sir Arthur Charles Clarke noted,

"Any sufficiently advanced technology is indistinguishable from magic."

What may appear to be real may be a distortion of reality due to some type of advanced technological ruse.

Feeling a little uneasy?

It's okay.

That's just the first step to recognizing our limitations as humans.

So, if determining ultimate reality may be difficult due to the limitations of our consciousness, especially as evidenced by all the conflicts as among various religious and a-religious groups, how can we become unified in our philosophical foundations with Libertarian Voluntaryism?

The answer there is that we start with how humans act.

If we know that, no matter what, people act as if they do exist in empirical reality, judge others based on physical evidence and argument, and have senses with which they engage others, we can start there as our foundation for building philosophy with empathetic reciprocity. If we assume that human beings exist as is acted upon performatively by action, we can then look at the nature of the human body in existence to think through what foundations are needed to move forward.

You know from your own experience that human beings require water, food, air, and shelter to survive. Without these fundamentals, people will die of dehydration, starvation, suffocation, and the harsh outdoor elements. If human beings require water, food, air, and shelter to survive, these things must be considered ethical to acquire and possess lest the very actors for which we are developing a philosophical framework for cease to exist in death.

How human beings develop an ethical code for this acquisition is a matter of positive adoption, that is, it's something thought about in the human psyche. It's a product of developed thought in the mind. What is developed in the mind then controls human action. What someone believes and how they perceive determines how they will act. To develop this philosophical reflection in your mind, we must first identify the parameters of your mental capacity.

First, let's talk about the concept of consent. Consent is the mental state of agreement or desire for a certain action. It's the idea that someone wants something to happen and that it should take place. How consent is manifested depends on the culture and language. Any English-speaking person knows that the word "Yes" signals agreement and consent to others. In another country like Japan, the word はい pronounced "Hai" signals the same. Different verbal articulations – same cultural meaning. The development of what makes effective consent is a core study of Libertarian Voluntaryist thought.

Generally, consent is thought to be able to be given on a sliding-scale basis from childhood leading to independent adulthood, with functioning adults being perceived as those able to give full consent. More on this topic will be developed in the chapters on "Parenting and Children" and "Common Objections with Answers and Explanations." For now, it can be recognized that consent is the foundation to ethical human interactions and that its manifestation has nuance and market recognition.

With this backdrop in mind, it can be noted that it is logically impossible to want one's consent to be violated. If you want something to happen, then you consent to it. You cannot "want" your consent to be infringed upon because the desire is the manifestation of the consent.

Which is precisely why "consent" is the ultimate basis for Libertarian Voluntaryist ethics. It is logically sound and is the mechanism by which people can demonstrate their desires to others.

Anything less than respect of consent leads to serious harms.

For example, if a woman does not consent to having sex, then someone forcing their will to have sex with her amounts to an act of rape, an act that is often violent as the victim tries to stop her body from being used. If someone does not consent to being punched, then the punch is an act of battery, a strike against the will of the victim. If someone does not consent to giving over their money, then the money's taking could be an act of robbery if a mugger points a gun and grabs a victim's wallet. As you can see, the nature of consent really is at the heart of what makes many violent crimes "crimes" in the legal landscape of many countries. And consent, being the key arbiter for ethical behavior, makes even more sense if we have a foundation of self-ownership as the core property right for all people.

So, what is self-ownership? **Self-ownership** is the idea that each person has the highest right over their own body. Self-ownership, in Libertarian Voluntaryist ethics, stems from the brain activity that controls the human body. While some may try to claim that self-ownership is a tautology depending on their belief about the nature of "self" and "consciousness," the reality is that the brain is the mechanism that asserts control over the body to the exclusion of others and it is the center from which consciousness expression springs.

These facts about the brain are observable and demonstrable.[1] As the brain is the source of memories and the controller of the body through electric signals, it is the crux of human action. In making self-ownership stem from human brain activity, it makes it much easier to manage the rest of the issues that spring from bodily property rights formation.

As the brain exerts control over the body, human slavery (total outright alienation) is not ethically possible. The reason why is that the body cannot be alienated from the brain's control in whole until death. It would be like trying to sell someone a car but refusing to get out of the driver's seat. However, parts of the body can be alienated from control while living, such as with donating an organ or selling plasma. If one voluntarily alienates a part away from brain activity, then that part is no longer being controlled by the brain.

If the body is owned by the human consciousness occupying it, then no one has a default higher right to that person's body and any interference can be properly labelled as an infringement on the individual's sovereign right to their body. And if a body is ethically owned, then it makes sense that body's owner will need to exert other forms of ownership to keep the body functioning. This is where the need for outer-body property rights comes in for the sake of survival. At a minimum, people occupy some scarce space on the planet. Their body takes up physical room, thus, it is imperative that the Libertarian Voluntaryist ethical system respect the need for land development so that people can subsist and survive.

How people acquire rights to land and resources is a topic for the next chapter.

PERFORMATIVE CONTRADICTION TEST

In the event someone wishes to critique any of these foundations, the performative contradiction test can be used to demonstrate that a person is being disingenuous about their claims. For example, if someone says there is no such thing as "self-ownership," you can tell them that you will stab their body wantonly. Most reasonable people will refuse and try to stop you, exercising a performative property right of control over their body. The very nature of this resistance is a performative contradiction because their actions demonstrate that they do exert the psychology of property rights over their body to stop an assailant. They are acting as "self-owners" by resisting the attack. This same process can be applied to any tenet of Libertarian Voluntaryist foundations to demonstrate inconsistencies from critics. Those who contradict themselves can be said to be estopped (stopped in performative contradiction) from proposing a claim or course of action that they themselves are in contradiction of.

CHAPTER CONCLUSION

In sum, the philosophical foundations for Libertarian Voluntaryism do not require belief in an ultimate truth of existence- only that you accept you exist in a physical, observable reality. Libertarian Voluntaryism does not require a belief in God or a lack of belief in God- it only requires that you live in accordance with consent and property rights ethics. Libertarian Voluntaryism does not require that you follow a certain mission for your life- it only demands that you act with non-aggression within the context of consent and property rights toward other people.

The reasons for why you'd want to adopt this ideology are wholly up to you.

Like any other belief system, you will not be struck by lightning if you do not follow the Libertarian Voluntaryist ethical system. No God will deliver swift punishment for your misdeeds with an announcement of what the proper conduct should have been upon your delinquency. Rather, it is up to you to find within yourself the empathetic reciprocity to be the change you want to see by stewarding a culture of peace through property rights for the next generation.

Those rewards are limitless.

3

PROPERTY RIGHTS

SCARCITY: THE PRECURSOR

Scarcity is the precursor to thinking about property rights because it is the point of conflict most present when people consider how their body and physical possessions are treated. For example, one can imagine a 1,000-foot by 1,000-foot piece of land with a beautiful beachfront view. There are not two pieces of land like it because, from where it sits, there cannot be a replication of that specific area – it is unique in space. Due to this limitation, people cannot all share that same spot at the same time without conflict over the space as it is too small to hold all people. In turn, there must be a shared psychology and management system to avoid physical conflict over this scarce resource.

Things that are not scarce cannot be considered property in the same manner. For example, if someone could replicate an apple you had without depriving you of your original apple, there would not be a concern because the apple possessed by you would be unchanged and you would still have your apple to use as you please. The duplication of this apple does not deprive the original ownership of the original material. While apple duplication may sound more like science fiction at the moment, a clearer example is the example of intellectual property by the state, that is, the notion that someone can own an idea put into fixed form to the exclusion of others.

As an idea can be replicated without depriving the inventor of their physical design, ideas and design methods from ideas are not in-and-of-themselves candidates for property rights. A person could manufacture their own microwave with their own property by copying another's design without depriving the inventor of their physical microwave invention. A person could copy an artist's drawing without depriving the artist of the original physical drawing. A person could copy a digital file without removing the digital content from the digital creator's storage device.

To claim otherwise is to make a claim that one person can control the wholly-independent property of another for an arbitrary period of time. For example, imagine one man makes a drawing of a new superhero character in Florida and posts the drawing online. Another artist sees this drawing and makes the same drawing using their own pencils and paper thousands of miles away in Indonesia. If the Florida man claims to own the idea of the drawing through intellectual property, then he is claiming that he can use violent force against the artist in Indonesia to stop him from making a replica or derivative work, even though the artist in Indonesia is using his own skills, paper, and pencils. In this manner, the Florida man would essentially be having a higher claim of ownership to the pencils and paper of the Indonesian artist. This imposition cannot be made without violating the sovereign property rights the Indonesian artist has in the pencils and papers that are justly his.

Any desire to be rewarded for innovation must not come from owning ideas and threatening others with violence but, rather, through coming up with market innovations for consensual market transaction. More about this topic can be found in the "Common Objections with Answers and Explanations" chapter and in *Against Intellectual Property* by Stephan Kinsella.[2]

DEFINITION OF PROPERTY

Property is a bundle of concepts held in human psychology, including the concepts of:

1.) Possession: Physical control.

2.) Usage: Use of the property to implement a function or not implement a function.

3.) Destruction: Making unusable.

4.) Exclusion: Keeping others from.

5.) Disposition: Selling, trading, gifting, or abandoning.

Property rights concepts applies to physical things (matter) as follows below:

THE FOUNDATION: SELF-OWNERSHIP

As noted in the last chapter, self-ownership is the concept that each human being owns their body and has the highest claim to it. This ownership stems from brain impulses being placed on the body which act as a controlling agent. If one accepts self-ownership stemming from brain activity, then it can be understood by observation that people tend to both involuntarily and voluntarily act in defense of themselves. Their white blood cells fight off infecting bodies and people use their hands, arms, legs, and feet to repel objects, creatures, or persons they do not wish to touch their body.

This observation of the natural, consistent application of self-ownership continues with accuracy to alienation of parts, whereby people can give up control of body parts by cutting off brain impulse activity. This takes place frequently with donation of blood and organs when people extract the tissue away from brain impulse and give it to another. Under this reasoning, the body cannot be given in whole until death, making the concept of slavery (total living human ownership) a logical impossibility. As long as the brain is exerting impulses, a claim of ownership is being made on the body.

Trying to alienate the body in whole while living would be as much of a farce as trying to sell a car but refusing to get out of the driver's seat. By not getting out, one is not truly giving up property rights and, thus, the alienation has not taken place. With these principles in mind, it becomes easy to delineate self-ownership for most all people save rare medical anomalies.

REAL PROPERTY (LAND)

Property norms for land are necessary as life itself demands it. Human beings take up space in time and require the conversion of natural resources for the body to survive. Thus, every human being must, at a bare minimum, both occupy some spot of land to the exclusion of others and capture and convert physical resources to continue the process of replenishing cells.

The key to consistent property ownership is making claims specific and clear to the notice of others. Traditionally, this kind of property development came in the form of homesteading: clearing land from the state of nature and

18

developing structures on top of it to exclude other humans and put them on notice as to the land's use. To avoid generalized claims like those in the state make, claims to land should be specific and well-defined with some sort of visible fencing and also cleared for building structures. Leaving land in the state of nature is antithetical to strong property norms as it makes it so that people could claim wide areas of land without ever having to perform any labor to capture and control it. By strictly adhering to a homesteading norm based on setting off land with physical markers and clearing it for construction, concerns about centralization of control and ambiguity of ownership can be largely avoided due to the construction required.

Those who attempt to allow their land to turn back into a state of nature run the risk of making it appear that the land has been abandoned. To avoid this, a market norm of development and fencing ought to be encouraged. This will not only lead to less confusion about the land's use, but it will also help prevent adverse possession, that is, one person developing onto the claimed land of another. A lack of clear fencing coupled with a lack of development makes it easy for a neighbor to accidentally build over.

Ownership of spaces should not be extended above or below land without physical construction to avoid generalized claims and to help make clear who owns what area by notice of development. This means that airspace is generally open to use unless physical construction into the sky privatizes the space. Construction underground is also possible, but it should be noted that any damage caused by those drilling underground could cause liability. For example, if a company tries building a tunnel for excavation underneath a person's home, and that tunnel causes damage to the home, the company can be held liable for the damage.

A means to helping reduce this problem is to have home construction come with boundary pole development whereby long poles are plunged underground to mark fencing in the same manner that one may fence in their yard to show claim of ownership.

Abandonment of land-based property should be made clear by removing barriers and posting notice of intent to abandon to avoid confusion.

CAPTURE

Capture takes place when something from the state of nature is physically taken out of it by a human. This could be taking an apple from an unowned tree or excavating minerals. When someone captures something from the state of nature (unowned) through physical means, they become the owner of the material/resource/creature.

ANIMALS

As animals fall outside of the Libertarian Voluntaryist ethical treatment application, animals may be captured out of the state of nature or consensually traded for in the same manner as one would take any other resource out of the state of nature and privatize it. More on the topic of animals can be found in the chapter, "THE TREATMENT OF ANIMALS."

SALE AND TRADE

A person who captures or homesteads property can voluntarily trade with others for other rightfully owned property. This can come in the form of selling/trading land or selling/trading unfinished and finished goods. So long as the transaction is based on consent and is not fraudulent (i.e. made by lying about an aspect of the deal to trick the other person into trading) then the property ownership changes status to the respective new owners.

CONCLUSION

While this chapter isn't exhaustive of all possible situations, it provides the barebones framework needed to consider how property rights can be reasonably metered to avoid conflicts as among humans. Any market-based agency that handles disputes would be wise to manage those disputes under this framework to avoid escalation of violence as among people.

4

THE NATURE OF THE STATE

T he nature of the state is a critical discourse for Libertarian Voluntaryism as the philosophy is specifically in defiance of statism. **Statism** is the idea that a person or group of persons can ethically claim to own wide areas of land and pre-existing people and structures by unilateral decree. Historically, statism began with tribes as tribal leaders started to exert control over those born into a small community. The first major state was Sumer in the historical region of southern Mesopotamia.[3] The governments of today that we are more familiar with are those which arose out of responses to monarchy in the 18th century, governments which attempted to remove the sole power of Kings and Queens in favor of shared power with nobles in Parliament and, later, power through democratic representatives.[4] No matter the form, every single state shares the quality that the rule was imposed by a select group of people at the exclusion of most everyone. For example, the United States Constitutional ratification participation was limited largely to white landowning males aged 21 and older, which excluded non-landowning white males, women, and minorities.[5] In this manner, governments have typically been comprised of those in economic and political power forcing everyone to accept their rule through fiat and force. How governments ultimately maintain power is through promises of spoils to those who would do violence on behalf of the political elite. Whether the political elite's power stems from hiring mercenaries or having a standing army paid for by promissory notes, those in the state use hired guards to enforce their rule and take from everyone at large to fund the enforcement.[6] Historically, this rule was often then claimed to be sanctioned by a God or the Gods, with a divine right proclamation used to scare the population into submission through mysticism.[7]

As governments do not rely on individual consent and force a rule upon all people by default of birth in a region, they cannot comport with the values of Libertarian Voluntaryism. Governments threaten violence against pre-existing people and property. The only way they could possibly move toward an ethical existence is if they are accepted and supported through individual consent from inception and ongoing.

Voting cannot be a substitute for this individual consent as voting is forced upon all people whether they agree with having a vote in the first place, or not. Voting is a ruse meant to make it appear that people have a choice in their rule when, in reality, both the establishment of the rule and the mechanism of the rule were forced onto all people. Voting defensively should not be taken as a sign of consent either. The Voluntaryist philosopher Lysander Spooner aptly noted that voting defensively to try to lessen oppression is like someone who has been kidnapped and forced into a battle not of their choosing.[8] That the kidnapped picks up a sword and fights other men trying to kill him is not evidence of his desire for the battle, but that he simply wishes to survive the fight and leave.

If still unsure of government's nature, think about yourself and your own abilities. Do you, as an individual, have the right to take from your neighbor by force, even if you gave what you took to a person in need? Does your neighbor have the right to do that to you? What if your neighbor got with 10 other neighbors and signed a paper saying that they could take from you to give to another? Ten not enough? How about, 100? 1,000? 10,000?

Would that then make it ethical?

If you agree that your neighbor cannot do that to you even if they got 10,000 signatures, and you could not do the same, then how can you delegate an ability you do not have to the government?

Simply, you cannot.

Which is why "democracy" is an obfuscation of reality. A government using "democracy" is really attempting to do things that individuals could not do on their own without being viewed as inherently unethical.

• You could not take from your neighbor by force without being labelled a "thief," but the government does this through taxation.

• You could not take your neighbor's land without being considered a squatter, but the government does this through eminent domain.

• You could not kidnap your neighbor and force them to labor for you, but the government does this through conscription.

- You could not shoot your neighbors because you did not like their lifestyle, but governments do this all the time under the banner of "war."

As you can see, the government does things in the name of a "common good" that you yourself could not ethically do on your own.

There is NO EXCEPTION for unethical behavior just because a group of people decide to call themselves "the state." The ethics of property rights and consent applies to all people in all situations for all time.

If you're asking yourself, "But without taxation, who will build the roads?"

Don't worry.

The next chapter is devoted to thinking about how common needs can be met ethically without taxation.

For further reading on the nature of the state, check out The Anatomy of the State by Murray N. Rothbard and The Most Dangerous Superstition by Larken Rose.

5

BUT WHO WILL BUILD THE ROADS?

But who will build the roads?!?!

This is one of the most common expressions people have when they first hear the claim that taxation by the state is inherently unethical. And it's no surprise. Most people spend their formative years in public school where they open each day with a pledge to the American flag and are subsequently bombarded with messages in their history classes about how, if it wasn't for the U.S. government, we would be poor, starving, and speaking Russian or Chinese.

The question of how infrastructure people use gets built and maintained in the absence of taxation is much simpler than one may realize. The first step is to think about yourself and your own human action. When it comes to meeting your needs, what do you do? Do you just sit on your hands and hope that someone comes to clothe and feed you? Maybe if you're an infant or a toddler, sure. But most all grown adults already understand that they are responsible for themselves. They must look both ways when crossing a street to avoid being hit. They must take a shower, put on a shirt and pants, and feed themselves. If they don't work, they won't have the resources to pay for needed things, like food, water, and housing.

When it comes to deciding what someone is going to do with their day, they use their reasoning skills to think about what they do and don't like. Typically, people do not seek out poor quality in their lives. They will seek out the opinions of friends and family and check out online reviews of various goods and services to consider what option is best for them. Millions upon millions of people do this every day, and they do so coordinating their time and labor despite there being millions upon millions of different options to choose from, from what one could wear, to what one could eat, to where one could travel.

When it comes to these needs, a central planner is not needed to survey what everyone wants to wear and eat that day. Each person can go out into the market and choose what it is they want based on the diversity of offerings from business owners attempting to attract customers and provide value.

The act of providing value to others is a natural incentive because, in doing so, people exchange their labor and goods for mutual benefit. The baker sells cakes to hungry customers, and the money the baker earns allows him to buy things from others that he wants, such as fruits and vegetables from the grocery store or gas for his car.

This natural incentive for people to trade is what incentivizes the creation of roads and any other mechanism by which people could offer value to others. Roads are not exempt from the same calculation that is made in making t-shirts. Most everyone wears t-shirts. Most everyone uses roads. But because the government has monopolized a large part of road construction, many are confused about what can be provided in a free market. And this occurs despite there being tons of private roads built, from roads built for common development communities to the private roads built in Disney World.

Even though private roads exist everywhere, it is difficult for people to imagine what roads could be like without state central planning. And this is because government monopolization hides what is possible in the market and confuses people on what could be provided if people are free to choose. If we have a free market in transportation, we might even see roads slowly become a thing of the past as air travel becomes more prominent.

Sadly, the U.S. government, through the FAA, shut down development of a ride-sharing program set to revolutionize shared private flight like Uber and Lyft did for road-based ride sharing.[9] What could that have looked like if it was allowed to flourish? We may not know for a while, but hopefully, one day we will.

In the past, we did not know what a freed market in cell phone electronics would create until the FAA's restrictions on building a cellular network were upended. Did you know that cell phones could have arisen 40 years earlier if it were not for the FAA stopping their development by limiting what bandwidths AT&T could use?[10] It's wild to think that people in the year 2000 could have been using smartphones already, but that's what's missed out on when the government monopolizes the control and determines who the winners and losers are.

So, if you're wondering who will build the roads, it's PEOPLE. People will build roads based on interest and demand in the same manner as people make t-shirts, cars, and pumpkin pie. How we get from where we are now with current road construction is a topic for the chapters of "COMMON OBJECTIONS WITH ANSWERS AND EXPLANATIONS" and "NOW HOW DO WE GET THERE?" For now, just know that stuff gets built because of the natural incentive for people to be rewarded in providing value to others, and this includes everything and anything people are willing to pay for voluntarily.

If you want to read more on how roads could be privatized and built going into the future, check out Walter Block's Book: *The Privatization of Roads and Highways* available on the Mises Institute Website here: https://mises.org/library/privatization-roads-and-highways

6

PARENTING AND CHILDREN

The treatment of children is often a difficult topic for many to navigate as children are largely unable to take care of themselves. As such, they are dependent on their parents for care, support, and wisdom to flourish eventually as functioning adults. As Libertarian Voluntaryists try to maximize consent and minimize the initiation of force, the respect of children's bodies and wills is an important consideration in fostering and reciprocating peace and love.

Of first importance is defining the relationship between parents and children. Children are not "owned" by their parents. This is because children are independent human beings who are exercising control over their bodies to the exclusion of others. Rather than defining the relationship as "ownership," Libertarian Voluntaryists consider the relationship to be a trust relationship where parents are acting as stewards of children until they are mature enough to take care of themselves without their parents' help.

As stewards, parents have the highest trust relationship for children as the biological norm. It is well-known that a child's biological parents have the closest connection because of the bio-chemical relationship fostered by a child and mother in utero.[11] A mother has the highest investment in the wellbeing of a child in that she has offered up her bodily resources and, thus, should be viewed as having the highest stewardship rights claim.

In this environment, parents may exercise their property rights for the sake of rearing a child in a healthy path. A parent can offer a child food, shelter, and companionship so long as those actions are not violating the physical body of a child in causing physical damage. A parent can refuse to provide unhealthy things to a child as well to ensure that a child is not harmed by something that he or she cannot handle.

In this realm, young children are not able to fully consent to all activities an adult can because they do not have the brain capacity to be able to understand what it is they are engaging in.[12] This is where the stewardship of the parent exists to help protect a child from poor choices or unknown risks and dangers.

A Libertarian Voluntaryist parent who wishes to help children build a strong foundation for independence so that their children can meaningfully consent one day ought to use peaceful parenting tactics based in reason and evidence as opposed to spanking, threats, and yelling. If you're not familiar with peaceful parenting, that is okay. For now, it can be summed as looking to use words and empathetic touch over threats and physical hitting to help children learn how to manage their thoughts, emotions, and bodily functions. You can see several books on how to be an effective peaceful parent and non-violent communicator at the end of this chapter.

Libertarian Voluntaryist parenting discipline, if required, is focused on removing rewards/good things rather than using hitting and threats. In this manner, Libertarian Voluntaryists seek to provide such a loving and building home environment that a child would want to behave in a peaceful manner to continue enjoying their fun activities.

A parent can stop a child's dangerous behavior through force, but this does not need to be escalated to hitting to help a child learn. For example, many mistakenly make a hyperbolic assertion that a parent cannot stop a child from touching a hot stove or running across a road with traffic because it stops the "will" of the child. This is a mistake of thinking that stems from not analyzing all property rights norms in the environment. At home, the stove belongs to the parent, and a parent has a property right to stop a child from touching a hot stove as it is their property. A parent could, in teaching a lesson, hold a child's hands above a hot stove if a child is curious while saying "hot" to communicate to a child the dangers of touching a stove. Likewise, a parent stopping a child from walking into a busy intersection is providing property rights defense for oncoming drivers as the child walking into their moving cars would be a violation of the drivers' property rights in their cars.

While describing a parent's right to stop a child from danger in property rights terms may seem a bit academic and pedantic to explore, it is an important analysis to build a consistent framework of philosophy so that the ethical treatment of children can be advanced. Eventually, when a young person is ready and able to leave out on their own, their journey into adulthood will be complete and social norms built on Libertarian Voluntaryist ethics will foster respect of a young person's decision to start their own independent life.

If you wish to build your own toolkit for helping children grow up in a peaceful and supportive home, please get and read the following books below:

Healing The Child Within: Discovery and Recovery for Adult Children of Dysfunctional Families Paperback by Charles L. Whitfield M.D.

Nonviolent Communication: A Language of Life, 3rd Edition: Life-Changing Tools for Healthy Relationships by Marshall B. Rosenberg Ph.D.

Peaceful Parent, Happy Kids: How to Stop Yelling and Start Connecting by Dr. Laura Markham.

EDUCATION AND SCHOOLING

In Libertarian Voluntaryist ethics, a child's education is not an owed property right, that is, a parent is not required to give a specific course of instruction to a child. However, the ethos of Libertarian Voluntaryism does set a backdrop for what kind of educational practices are unethical.

Compulsory public schooling is inherently unethical as it is a product of state central planning. Compulsory public school is rooted in Prussian militarism, developed to create soldiers who would be willing to die on the battlefield.[13] Later, it was adopted by other European and North American governments as a means of producing factory workers and ridding native populations of their culture by colonizing their children.

A big misconception of compulsory public school is that it is meant to give children "basic skills" so they can be functioning, literate adults. The actual core of the compulsory schooling ethos is unyielding obedience marked by grades and grade levels. Grades are signals that a child is both willing and able to conform to the dictates of the teacher and to quiet their other interests, dreams, and aspirations. You can reflect on this for yourself in thinking through the schooling process. If a child knows the material, but refuses to turn in homework, they get an "F" or "Failure" mark. The knowledge is not what is sought, but the performance in turn-in. If a child is reading in class, but the book is not on-topic for what the teacher wants, the teacher confiscates the book because it is a "distraction." In this way, what is valued is not a child's interest in reading but rather a child's conformity to whatever a teacher demands of them in a forced environment.

This type of control is amplified over time as children are segregated into honors and regular classes. Children are given rewards and privileges such as sports participation or field trip participation only upon reaching a sufficient grade point average and maintaining a lack of detention slips.

By the time schooling is complete, children are often unable to motivate and direct themselves. They have become wholly dependent on waiting to hear from an adult what they should do. They have internalized shame, so extreme, they will even shame others for criticizing the schooling system even if they themselves feel harmed by it.

THE ETHICAL ALTERNATIVE: SELF-DIRECTED EDUCATION

The most ethical form of education from the Libertarian Voluntaryist ethos is "unschooling" or "self-directed education." With self-directed education, adults act as facilitators instead of performance judges as children are free

34

to choose their learning paths. Adults help children learn to read, write, and perform arithmetic as applies to their interests. In this way, adults foster the innate curiosities of children and help them naturally direct their own drive in learning. This can take place in many settings, such as with homeschooling, within a homeschooling cooperative, or at a self-directed learning center where the facility is run by several adults providing a self-directed environment.

One such example of a formal self-directed learning center is the Sudbury Valley School in Framingham, Massachusetts.[14] Since 1968, students there ranging in ages from 4 to 19 have enjoyed educational freedom on a beautiful campus that includes a kitchen, music room, arts and crafts room, and outdoor space. Just like anyone going to a regular public school, the students graduate to a variety of endeavors, from working a job right after graduation to attending top-tier colleges and universities.

Self-directed learning does not mean that there are never any textbooks, formal classes, or boundaries. Rather, it means that a child has the choice to use a textbook as desired, a choice to enroll in a formal class if desired, and the responsibility of respecting property rights boundaries of others in their learning.

Exiting the compulsory schooling paradigm is one of the most difficult psychological practices because of how long the programming lasts for. It's hard to imagine what life could be like otherwise when someone has just spent 13 years in compulsory schooling, possibly followed with another 4 or 5 in a college that in many ways mirrored public school.

To help you understand the history of compulsory school and what healthy Unschooling looks like, I recommend you read the following books:

The Underground History of American Education: A School Teacher's Intimate Investigation Into the Problem of Modern Schooling by John Taylor Gatto.

Dumbing Us Down: The Hidden Curriculum of Compulsory Schooling by John Taylor Gatto.

Unschooled: Raising Curious, Well-Educated Children Outside the Conventional Classroom by Kerry McDonald.

Free to Learn: Why Unleashing the Instinct to Play Will Make Our Children Happier, More Self-Reliant, and Better Students for Life by Peter Gray.

ABORTION

The topic of abortion is a heated subject that has been debated by philosophers for centuries. While many people focus more on the end results for analysis, the principled Libertarian Voluntaryist first must analyze the situation from inception and apply the core philosophical principles to the entire process that leads to children being born.

In doing so, it becomes much easier to balance the negative rights of the mother and child without creating contradictory assertions and unlimited duties.

To properly analyze the situation, we must first look at the nature of conception itself. Pre-existing humans came to be through the evolution of organisms over time. Without reproduction, there are no humans to even have a philosophical discourse about. If no one reproduces, within a generation, all humans would die off. Seeing this fact sets the groundwork that reproductive action is a biological function and a predicate to existence.

Next, we must look at the nature of conception and how that fits within the non-aggression principle ethic. As Libertarian Voluntaryists seek to maximize consent and minimize the initiation of force, it becomes difficult to tackle the nature of conception as children are created without their consent. It is physically impossible (as far as we know) to gain consent from a conscious being before they have consciousness with which to consent.

Which would mean that, if we hold the N.A.P. standard to conception, it would justify stopping parents from procreating as their action forces a child to come to life without their consent. This absurdity cannot be metered without reaching a nihilistic, anti-human end where humans would eventually go extinct if kept from procreating on the notion that a child cannot consent to being created. To avoid this self-defeating conclusion, the act of conception should be considered in-and-of-itself a biological process that is a-moral, much like the act of having blood in the body or breathing air. As conception is itself a necessary predicate to existence and human life, the N.A.P. analysis cannot be applied to it as it would lead to human extinction.

With this in mind, arguments about parents choosing to have sex and, thus, being held responsible for a child's existence as a unilateral duty can be rejected. If unnerved by this rejection, we can look at what applying the N.A.P. to conception would look like for the other absurd results in consequence.

1.) If procreation creates a duty-causing violation, then people would be justified in using defensive force to stop would-be parents from procreating.

2.) If procreation creates a duty-causing violation, then parents can be held as indentured servants to their child for their child's life as the N.A.P. violation is life-long.

3.) If procreation creates a duty-causing violation, people are justified in investigating whether a woman's miscarriage was caused by the woman, either by intentional force or by negligent or reckless behavior.

4.) If procreation creates a duty-causing violation, and a mother has an abortion, that woman could be killed for their violation under estoppel as women cannot claim that they should not be killed if they themselves murder.

5.) If procreation creates a duty-causing violation, then people can use physical force to compel a mother to provide whatever a child demands, as there is no minimum or maximum standard of care to limit what a parent should be providing save the victim's demands.

As you can see, the idea of holding a parent as having a duty to a child because of a unilateral responsibility from "forcing" a child to exist would create some bizarre situations that would encourage force being used against mothers and fathers.

In addition to these deductive conclusions, it is also important to note the current biological conditions of mothers in procreation. Miscarriage, a biological eviction, currently takes place in 20-30% of conceptions depending on access to medical care.[15] Because of this, one should also consider the fact that attempting to have a child is itself a risk of a child dying. Put into perspective, this 1-in-5 chance of miscarriage would be akin to running over and killing a child unintentionally 1-in-5 days of going to work. Would most people drive cars to work if one day each week they ran over and killed a child?

Probably not.

Yet, this takes place in millions of iterations as billions of people around the world have sex and, in many cases, conceive but then lose the child. While some people try to suggest miscarriage is a special situation as it is not necessarily chosen, one should recognize that miscarriage risks are known and that a woman could reduce miscarriage risk or choose not to procreate should the risk be too high.

Some factors that increase miscarriage rates includes obesity, weak uterine lining, and unhealthy food and drink choices. Women who have had a prior miscarriage are also at a significantly higher risk for future miscarriage as well. So, if in other areas of life, risky behavior can make someone considered liable for unintended consequences, why would the act of procreation receive special pleading?

For example, driving and texting (distracted driving) is a known risk that can lead to someone's death if they are run over. If someone was distracted while driving and hit a child, killing that child, they would be considered negligent or reckless in causing that child's death, even if they did not intend it. To be consistent, women who attempt to procreate with known risks, and whose attempts lead to miscarriage, should be held liable if holding a strict N.A.P. standard.

Few, if any, proponents who consider abortion outright "murder" hold this standard. Instead, they attempt to downplay the risks and outcomes of attempted procreation while holding women to a standard of care only if their mind wishes for the abortion/eviction to take place.

Between the inherent risk of miscarriage and the focus on not causing infant death, one would expect that a robust application of the N.A.P. to procreation would put a duty on women to only attempt procreation if they are healthy enough to do so with minimal risk. This standard is not generally held and, thus, should be another factor in rejecting the argument of anyone trying to suggest that abortion/eviction is always outright murder. If one is unwilling to place a duty of care on a mother to not procreate if there is risk, but they will put a duty of care for other activities that can lead to unintended deaths, then they are hypocrites.

So, what then is the ethical conclusion about what a mother could do with a child in her body?

For the sake of argument, we can assume that a child should be considered a full human being at the point of conception. This helps to eliminate any ambiguity and gives the most favorable position to respecting the body and property rights of a conceived child. It's also a reasonable position to take as all the genetic information for a child is present when the egg meets sperm and the process of cellular division begins. Given a most-favorable light position to a child in the womb, one can then analyze how to meter out the hierarchy of property rights and self-ownership. As the mother pre-exists the child, and the child only comes into existence through the grace of the mother's continued supply of blood and nutrients, it should be noted that the mother's claim to her own body is at a higher right of claim than a child's. A child cannot be owed a duty and a right to the mother's bodily resources as this would be a forcible taking of the mother's bodily resources.

Any attempt to create an analogy to this situation with third parties fails for a lack of true similarity. For example, some suggest an analogy to conception with someone who accidentally ends up on an airplane. The person who ends up on the plane may have drunkenly stumbled into the plane or may have been a worker who was knocked unconscious by a falling suitcase while putting bags into the plane. Someone unwittingly ending up on a plane is not analogous to conception and child carriage as a child's existence is wholly predicated on the actions and body of the mother, unlike a stranger caught in someone else's property.

This is important to remember as the argument for suggesting a duty to a child can also be conversely argued in similar fashion of a child owing a duty to a mother and father. It could be said that, as a child's life is formed from property of a mother's body, that the child should be the mother's property or, at least, "owe" his or her parents for life. This should be rejected for the aforementioned idea of considering conception a-moral to avoid unlimited, unilateral duties and, as well, for the logical absurdity of outright human ownership (as explained in the PROPERTY RIGHTS chapter).

41

Looking at the mother and child's independent rights to their bodily property and the existing hierarchy, it can be argued that a mother has the right to remove the child from her body. Libertarian scholar Walter Block has called this process "evictionism."[16] However, unlike Block's position, I do not argue that a mother has a duty to pay for and use life-sustaining technology to keep a child alive. Rather, a mother has a right to expel a child from her body and, if that child dies in the process, such is a consequence of the exercising of said rights. While I do not personally find this to be an admirable thing, it is an important consistency to hold to avoid rationalizing other people escalating violence against mothers.

To uphold the Libertarian Voluntaryist prongs of maximizing consent and minimizing the initiation of force, a mother should avoid going out of her way to kill a child i.e. killing a child as a focus rather than as a result. Where this comes into play most clearly is where a mother is nearing term and the eviction of a child would still leave a child alive outside the womb. Killing a child intentionally, such as with using scissors or a vacuum on the way out, should be considered an escalation of violence as it goes beyond removal. In sum, killing a child who would otherwise survive the removal process would be a violation of the child's bodily property rights.

What this standard does is permit respect of a mother's bodily property right to expel unwanted persons from her body while also respecting the idea that other human beings should not intentionally kill a child outside of the removal process. In tandem with this, a mother has a negative duty to not harm a child physically beyond removal and, thus, a mother cannot forcibly keep a child from care offered by others. Holding this standard both avoids imposing a duty on a mother to provide care but also permits the opportunity for a child to receive charitable care from willing persons.

The reason why this standard is wise to maintain beyond the deductions from establishing property right hierarchies is to recognize that unwilling mothers are going to be problematic in how a child is treated. Forcing motherhood on an unwilling mother would likely have serious consequences for how a child is cared for growing up due to neglect and abuse. Further, any deviation from this reciprocal standard would also rationalize physical, violent force being used against a mother to both take care of a child prenatally and after a child is born.

Anyone who tries to impose a duty but who will not articulate a standard of care for how a child should be treated before and after birth and, for what duration, is trying to hide behind ambiguities. They have no skin in the philosophical game for a "compared to what" of what a mother should do for her child to not be considered negligent and for how long she should offer care to not be considered abusive.

Continuing with this line of thought provides a clear framework that parents should not be held to a standard of care outside of N.A.P. thinism and that children, likewise, cannot be forced to remain with parents who are hurting them through physical violence or starvation. This makes the most sense when one internalizes that "good parenting," whatever that may entail depending on the social sphere, cannot be forced without creating more opportunities for physical violence against both parents and children who are threatened to conform to some amorphous outside social sphere of "right" or "wrong" parenting styles.

With education and technology, abortion and eviction can be reduced trending toward zero. This requires a change in culture where people are actively thinking about how to respect the bodies and properties of others so that they can grow in empathy and prudence. Rationalizing more opportunities for violence against women exerting their bodily property rights is only going to lead to a rationalization for interventionism and spying on women and their families.

ADDITIONAL NOTE: A common counter-argument some try to levy is that even though a mother has no duty to a child in providing sustenance, a mother has a fixed duty to not kill the child in eviction. The contradiction in this thinking is exposed when one counters that a mother could cut her umbilical/nuchal cord, which would cause the child to die due to lack of blood flow. Most often in response, the counter-arguer will suggest that the mother cannot do this because it will cause the child to die. Suggesting that a mother could not sever her own body part (her property) to stop her own blood (her property) from flowing is itself an imposition of a forcible, unilateral duty to give up her body's resources as well as a claim of ownership to her blood and tissue. This imposition debunks the original statement that a mother has no duty to give sustenance to a child. The argument that a mother cannot remove a child because a child may die becomes moot at this point because the claimant now is clearly trying to impose duties onto the mother to force her to provide her blood and connection to a child regardless of eviction/abortion outcomes. If being consistent, a child who dies because of cut-off blood flow is experiencing the inevitably similar outcome of evicting a child from the womb who dies while being cut off from the umbilical cord and mother's blood flow.

7

DISPUTE RESOLUTION AND JUSTICE

Dispute resolution in a freed market, that is, one that is defined by adhering to Libertarian Voluntaryist norms, will depend on the market choices of individuals. It would be difficult to say exactly how it would manifest in the same way that George Washington would have trouble saying what the latest iPhone in 2020 could look like from the vantage of the 1700s. Predicting the future when the opportunities are limitless can be difficult. However, we can think about a few ethical foundations with dispute resolution and justice and how that could shape what it ultimately looks like.

Libertarian Voluntaryism is firstly about reducing conflict among humans and making them whole when harm takes place. As such, the goal of a Libertarian Voluntaryist justice system would be to make whole harmed parties as best as possible to bring back a state of what was before being disrupted.

CIVIL HARMS

When it comes to civil harms, that is, disputes over contracts, accidents, and other acts of property harm that may not be intended by the offender, the goal should be to make whole the harmed party and to position them as they would have been had they not been infringed upon or if their contract was fulfilled. To the extent that something cannot be replaced due to uniqueness, like a rare car, monetary damages can be substituted.

If the contract broken is one of specific performance, such as an agreement that a singer sing at a concert, forcing a performance would be unethical if the party still does not want to perform. It could also potentially lead to more conflict with quality of work from a disgruntled performer. In this case as well, pecuniary relief is the substitute goal where specific performance would lead to forced labor and a conflict of interest. If someone is owed a physical object, then the object should be taken and given over where owed, such as where someone pays for a boat and the boat is not delivered as required. It is also possible that, if both parties agree, the victim and the offender could come to an agreement and settle how they wish to resolve the dispute after liability has been grounded in a court or other arbitration proceeding.

CRIMINAL HARM

In Libertarian Voluntaryist norms, if there is no victim, there is no crime. That's to say that criminal acts can only be defined as those where one person intentionally and knowingly does physical harm to the body or other physical property of another person.

Criminal harm takes place when an offender intentionally causes property harm to another, whether it's stealing something or beating up a person for the sake of intimidating them. In America, retributive justice, or the idea that an offender needs to have punishment independent of curing the victim, is relatively normalized in the culture as compared to many European countries.[17] Retribution, punishment for the sake of punishment, should be avoided in favor of restorative justice and rehabilitation. The goal should be to facilitate the offender's making whole the harmed party and to enhance, not hinder, their ability to do so and lead an ethical life going forward. While intentional acts of harm have more serious penalties, justice should still be focused on the restitution and rehabilitation to help end the cycle of victimization.

Prison, defined as imprisonment of one year or more, should be discarded as a lingering practice of statism. Keeping someone imprisoned for years does not help them afford restitution, nor does it get them prepared to live a non-criminal life. The effects of long-term imprisonment can be devastating psychologically and can ultimately make it more difficult for someone to acclimate to a non-violent life afterward.[18] Those who commit acts of violence should be held in a secure area only as is needed to prevent further harm being committed by the violent offender. While incarcerated, the offender should be rehabilitated with counseling, should the offender accept rehabilitation. If a person is so dangerous, and the harm so grave, that they cannot be trusted with freedom, or they refuse rehabilitation, then banishment would be a better means to dealing with them over prison due to the costs of upkeep.

A theoretical solution for removal is that those who are convicted of violent acts so egregious that their removal is appropriate, such as with acts of murder, serial rape, and child molestation, should be dropped off on a primitive island to live a primitive life, should they survive. Those who are convicted could have a one-year exoneration period, that is, a year for unexpected evidence to come in before they are

48

dropped off onto the remote island. This is not a mandatory conclusion, but merely a theoretical suggestion of what could be done to move toward less dependence on imprisonment.

Ultimately, what we could see change in time will depend on what kind of transition takes place. If we see a transition that starts within existing government structures, we may see the market in civil dispute resolution accelerate first and demonstrate what alternatives could be achieved. Over time, that could be applied to criminal harms in a criminal justice system rid of all **victimless crimes**, that is, rid of all criminal statutes that do not involve a person infringing on the physical body or property of another or defrauding another.

It's possible to imagine that market-based means may even incentivize transparency and resolution in financially sustainable ways, such as two affected parties choosing to appear in a televised arbitration court where their appearances are paid for by the court. Advertisers could support the court T.V. show, and the money that would be given to the participants from the show can act as potential judgement payment for the affected party. For example, imagine a person goes to T.V. court over a phone allegedly stolen by a supposed friend. The accused (the defendant) goes along with them to the T.V. appearance because they will be paid $1,000 for their appearance. If the defendant loses the case, the T.V. show can pay the plaintiff (the person suing) out of the monies that would have gone to the defendant. This provides public transparency and a restitution opportunity. Could the show be gamed? Sure. But that's where the T.V. show producers could come in to help curtail gaming, such as requiring that an official police report was filed under oath first before coming onto the T.V. show to arbitrate the dispute.

Again, this is just a theoretical suggestion of what could be possible. It's not necessarily what would arise given all the possible ways people working together in a freed market could improve dispute resolution.

If you're worried about laws being arbitrary and capricious in a freed market, I highly recommend reading the law review article, The Myth of the Rule of Law, by Georgetown law professor, John Hasnas, for a comparative to what exists now. He does a great job explaining in specific detail why the "Rule of Law" concept is a myth in practice and why a market in laws would not necessarily be more disorderly and unjust. Professor David D. Friedman, son of famed economist Milton Friedman, also explains how effective market-based laws can arise in his books, The Machinery of Freedom, and Law's Order: What Economics Has to Do with Law and Why It Matters.

More on what could take place in transition is touched on in the chapter, "NOW HOW DO WE GET THERE?"

8

THE TREATMENT OF ANIMALS

Libertarian Voluntaryist philosophy naturally revolves around human beings and their interactions because, by-and-large, it is human beings who are coming up with the concepts of property rights and applying those concepts in social and market norms. Despite this being the normal relationship dynamic, some people wish to extend the Libertarian Voluntaryist ethic and, of specific concern, the non-aggression principle, to species outside of homo sapiens. This chapter demonstrates why Libertarian Voluntaryist values cannot be extended to animals and, in tandem, offers a methodology of what it takes to foster a consistent application of Libertarian Voluntaryist norms.

First, Libertarian Voluntaryist norms applying to humans does not need to have argumentation to support it outside of axiom. One could assume the set of actors (human beings) and simply apply the principles as a positivism as human beings are the ones who are acting on the principles and are the class of organisms looking to communicate and apply these principles among themselves.

However, we can also produce a meaningful, logical framework that not only shows why human beings should be the only species considered (given known lifeforms), but the problematic consequences of attempting to apply the N.A.P. to other organisms that do not have the intellectual capacity of human beings. The primary reason why human beings are the subject class for Libertarian Voluntaryist ethics is that human beings are generally viewed as having the capacity to understand and reciprocate property rights. This is a crucial feature because any system of ethics where the subject class of actors cannot meaningfully hold the tenets will soon fall into violent chaos.

Take an extreme case to see what this means. For example, if I were to come up with an ethical rule/principle that stated, "It is unethical for human beings to breathe air," this would be rather problematic. If held consistently, all human beings would immediately begin to suffocate and, within minutes, die off. As can be seen, coming up with an ethical rule that causes all or most all members within a group to immediately perish would be problematic as those members cannot reasonably be expected to uphold the rule or they will die.

Likewise, creating and applying ethical rules that would inherently be broken to an extreme degree is also poor philosophy as people will then either suffer or be subject to punishment for breaking rules they inherently are going to break. If people cannot be expected to uphold certain ethical rules, then they cannot be held liable for their actions, no more than a fish could be found at fault for swimming or a baby be blamed for burping. When it comes to the non-aggression principle, Libertarian Voluntaryists have the expectation that people at large are at least capable of respecting the physical bodies and the physical properties of others. This expectation and ability to reciprocate is what underpins the psychological drive of "justice" and "responsibility" for human action.

Within the whole of human diversity, there are those who are unable to understand and reciprocate norms due to developmental stage, like young children, and those who cannot understand due to biological dysfunction such as those suffering Alzheimer's or those with Down Syndrome.

To accommodate for this diversity, the principle for species-wide reciprocity should be executed for application when the average member of a species is capable of understanding and reciprocating respect of other people's bodies and properties. Human beings have the brain size and raw intelligence for this kind of understanding that most all animals simply do not have. To further see why the "average member" metric is important, consider what the world would look like if most people could NOT understand and reciprocate some form of property rights. In that world, people would be taking things from others, destroying other's property, and causing physical harm at large to others through rape, battery, and murder. Such a world would be littered with violence beyond imagination, and even philosophy would be ignored to focus on fighting for survival against a brutal horde of human predators. In such a world, there would be so many violations, that people would essentially be focused on protecting themselves and exacting retribution for violations of their body and property.

Thankfully, we live in a world where most people can maintain some semblance of respect of body and property. Largely, people only make exceptions to this expectation when it comes to rationalizations of proxy violence through the state. Animals, on the other hand, do not have the ability to internalize and act on property rights to any meaningful degree. Carnivores would, categorically, be engaged in the business of committing violations against other living creatures. Herbivores would, by nature, violate physical property norms and even some standards of recklessness and negligence in accidentally killing other creatures they step on. Because of this, we can see absurdities emerge in applying the non-aggression principle to animals.

First, human beings would be justified in stopping all carnivores from eating other animals. They would even be able to use deadly self-defense on behalf of herbivores. This would lead to a kind of eugenics for carnivorous animals until they go extinct, disrupting the ecosystem dramatically.

Secondly, applying the N.A.P. to animals as against humans would also produce a justification for human beings to use force, even deadly force, against other humans for violating the bodies or "properties" of animals. A human being killing an animal for food or clothing would be viewed as a murderer meriting punishment.

Any attempt to craft special categories for animals as compared to humans would inherently create special pleading. For example, if one rationalizes carnivores eating other animals, then one could not really suggest that they are upholding the N.A.P. for animals as they are permitting violations to happen for one group, but not another.

Trying to use the term "need" puts the cart before the horse biologically as well, as all living things are evolutionary products of their environment and a "need" to eat living organisms is itself a product of genetic gravitation from survival selection of food source.[19] In simpler terms, the very reason why there are carnivorous organisms is because some creatures long ago were able to eat other organisms and then become dependent on that kind of nutrition with adaptation over time. To rationalize carnivorous animal activity is to put a stamp of approval on continuing the genetic dependence of killing other animals for food. If this same property were to be reciprocated to humans, human beings could not have arisen as they are a product of eating meat, which was what allowed humans to grow such a large brain size in the first place. Holding different standards for carnivorous creatures here commits a special pleading and, thus, should be rejected outright for being inconsistent with the supposed first intent of trying to end the killing of animals through the application of the N.A.P.

One can also readily see that the expectation of reciprocity is not consistently held for animals. To see this in concrete terms, it can be understood that human beings can be expected to not step on or drive over other humans. To do so typically imports a kind of negligent or reckless behavior analysis. However, human beings regularly kill and maim other creatures, from hitting them with planes, trains, and automobiles, to killing and displacing them in the construction of homes and roads. Outside the sophistry of state violence, people at large would not rationalize killing thousands of humans by steamrolling them over to pave a road or build an apartment complex. And, if they did at first, they would likely backtrack upon performing a comparative test where the killing involved themselves and their loved ones instead of strangers.

The very fundamental nature of human existence comes from the ingestion and killing of other animals in a manner that cannot be meaningfully abated or stopped without causing mass starvation and/or death to humans for their otherwise mundane activity. If each person was held accountable for any animal he or she killed, directly or indirectly through use of modern facilities, they would be worthy of the death penalty or a life sentence for the death they have brought to other living things.

As was noted before, any ethical rule which quickly leads to justification for mass violence and death or an extinction or near-extinction level of a species is a principle which ought to be rejected lest there are no more actors left to even engage with the philosophy. Anyone trying to suggest that animals could be treated with respect on a different scale is then also devolving away from the original premise of applying the N.A.P. to animals. Again, by holding two different standards between animals and humans, the proponent is now trying to create an apartheid system of ethics where human beings are treated more harshly for the same actions taken by other animals in the wild. Why should force be permitted to stop a human from eating deer, but not a lion? This cannot be answered without abandoning a consistent application of the non-aggression principle through creating a two-tiered ethics system.

Ultimately, what this means is that human beings cannot, and should not, use force against other humans for their actions against animals at large. Rather, animals should be treated under the property rights ethic of privatization until it can be shown that the average member of a particular species is capable of understanding and reciprocating property rights.

Should there be an exceptionally intelligent animal, that particular creature could be considered a moral agent exception to the rule. However, this is something that is more likely relegated to science fiction than a meaningful, present-day concern. If people wish for the treatment of animals to change, that must come through voluntary social norms in changing minds – not through physical violence - whether done through a private actor or someone acting under the auspices of "the state." Any other standard will inherently lead to human beings enacting violence against other human beings for participating in activities that are already rampant in nature and are not going to be meaningfully stopped by the people who supposedly care about animal wellbeing.

Remember that the aim of Libertarian Voluntaryism is to maximize consent and minimize the initiation of force as among humans, so any principle that would validate human-on-human violence where a human is not violating the property or body of another human will only amplify the discord as among humans.

9

COMMON OBJECTIONS WITH ANSWERS AND EXPLANATIONS

OBJECTION 1: But wouldn't warlords take over?

The objection that "warlords" would take over if the government could no longer be funded by taxes is especially comedic where the American government has been at war for over 90 percent of its existence.[20] The reality is that governments are warlords who both engage in wars abroad, such as with the War on Terror, to wars on the domestic population such as with the War on Drugs and the War on Covid. In the 20th century alone, over 260 million people were killed in state democide, which is more than the number of people killed in private acts of murder.[21] Warlords would not be taking over so much as changing positions, as has been the case for governments throughout the centuries. Ending "warlords" is precisely a product of people adopting Libertarian Voluntaryist ethics and no longer accepting that governments can engage in war in the same way that, privately, few would accept warlords trying to pillage and take over their local city.

OBJECTION 2: But what about dealing with past harms from the state?

A common criticism of Libertarian Voluntaryists from the Communist lens is that Libertarian Voluntaryists cannot adequately deal with the harms of governments past in how governments have wrongly benefitted certain people. The Communist obfuscates reality with their criticism because they do not intend to rectify all past harms, not that they even could as it is not possible to account for all acts of violence throughout human history and how that may have privileged some versus others through time.

As it is not possible to account for all past harms from different governments and other bad actors, we can only deal with present reality and still-existing actors. The Libertarian Voluntaryist seeks justice by ending the structures that continue to oppress us through state theft and victimless crime laws. We do not seek a state-based, forceful reorganization of society because that would itself also create more victims in the process in relying on state force to pick winners and losers. Unlike Libertarian Voluntaryists, the Communist attempts to tear down everything and start anew by slaughtering all those labeled as "capitalists." They then call for a reorganization of the economy via state central planning, with all property and businesses becoming collectively owned and managed via democracy. The Libertarian Voluntaryist rejects this solution as it creates new conflicts over scarce resources and indiscriminately meters violence against people whose "crime" was offering jobs paid in wages and owning a business, both of which are not ethical violations in themselves. Libertarian Voluntaryists know that, as not every past harm can be fixed ethically, the only ethical path forward is ending the present harms while trying to bring restitution for existing harmed parties. The creation of an ethical future comes as we move away from state-based solutions. For more on this topic, read the final chapter, "NOW HOW DO WE GET THERE?"

OBJECTION 3: But what about pollution?

POLLUTION DEFINED

"Pollution" is the wrongful damaging of physical bodies or properties through the release of some chemical agent, physical object, vibration, or radiation. "Pollution" in Libertarian Voluntaryist terms must be tied to a discreet actor proximately causing a discreet harm. For example, if the owner of a chemical plant ordered that a toxic chemical be dumped onto land owned by the company, and that toxic chemical leaks out onto someone else's land and causes bodily harm to others, then "pollution" in this sense is a proper label.

The toxic chemical is causing discreet damage to others' bodies and properties and the causation is connected directly to the actions of the company not securing toxic agents.

The same idea would apply to any other form of littering or dumping where the product is trespassing upon the property of another. The act of putting trash onto another's property without consent is the act of a physical intrusion and a violation of the non-aggression principle. This would include aggregate particulate, for example, a build-up of smog on others' homes. If an industrial plant releases ash, and that ash is building up on nearby homes, then the ash is itself the physical object that is violating the property rights of others and is causing property damage to homes.

The colloquial of "noise pollution" may only be considered a harm to the extent the sound is physically damaging a body or property. As sound is the vibration of air molecules, sound that causes actual physical damage would be comparable to someone throwing a baseball and that baseball hitting something or someone and causing physical damage. If the sound is simply a nuisance, but is not actually causing physical harm, then the sound issues must be otherwise dealt with via property rights choices, such as through insulation, community rules in apartment housing, or through intentionally choosing to live on land that has a greater separation from others.

The same analysis would apply to radiation, as radiation could only be a harm to the extent it is directly causing damage to bodies or properties. This would depend on differences in wave strength, as radio waves are typically not damaging whereas gamma radiation is.

THE LABEL OF "POLLUTION" CANNOT BE COMMON EXPERIENCE

Nothing can be "pollution" in Libertarian Voluntaryist terms that is itself a product of common use. For a good example, CO_2 as a "greenhouse gas." CO_2 cannot be considered a discreet harm because all people participate in its creation, at a bare minimum, just by breathing out, and participate in its productive use in mass industrialization. If people wish to no longer produce a particular byproduct that virtually all participate in, then that must come about through voluntary human action via convincing others to not produce or use the product.

Anything labelled as "pollution" that is not itself a property rights violation cannot be accurately labelled as such. For example, environmental extremists may claim that the act of making cars is itself "pollution" because it "hurts the earth," but that is not the case to the extent that the construction of a car is not violating the specific property rights of individuals' body or property.

POLLUTION REFINED

By tying the concept of pollution to discreet, physical intrusions with discreet, physical harms, it helps to delineate who is specifically causing what harm and what must be done to alleviate the harm. Through robust respect of property rights, individuals can choose their tolerances and hold those who do cause physical harm accountable.

REALWORLD COMPARISON

Now that we have that backdrop, it's important to look at the "compared-to-what" of the current landscape. In the world now, governments tend to act hypocritically when it comes to pollution and do not, even as among each other, hold the same standards. The U.S. military is one of the largest polluters by the descriptions given prior and by those who think carbon emissions are unfavorable for climate.[22] The U.S. government caps liability for polluters, such as capping BP's liability in the Deepwater Horizon oil spill of 2010.[23] The U.S. government has also been responsible for mass pollution events, such as with the EPA releasing 3 million gallons of contaminated water into the Animas River of southwest Colorado.[24]

Other countries share similar problems.

China has had some of the most polluted cities in the world while going through their industrial revolution, and the government there has often given companies permission to pollute through discharge fees and taxes.[25] So, as you can see, just because there are "governments," it does not mean that pollution is completely eradicated or consistently handled.

The focus then is to remind others that strong property rights permit individuals the opportunity to rectify harms and incentivize people to take care of what they own so they do not pollute. In doing so, solutions can arise in the free market from people voluntarily tackling pollution.

Take for example Boyan Slat's garbage capturing device that removes trash from the ocean without hurting sea creatures.[26] In his late teens and early 20s, he raised over 30 million dollars for his device and has successfully finished early prototype testing. His improved system captured 60 giant bags of waste to recycle, and he is continuing to refine his designs for more applications.

Through strong, individual property rights, and holding companies and individuals accountable for their harms, a free market approach to dealing with pollution can and will succeed.

OBJECTION 4: But what about viruses and vaccines?

The debate about vaccines, immunity, and risk to others is often a complicated topic as there is so much information to digest from ethics, to biology, to risk factors. For the principled Libertarian Voluntaryist, the question of vaccination is one that is readily answered by going to the root of what vaccination is as relates to individuals and property rights.

First, it's important to understand what vaccination is and what it is not. Vaccination in modern times is typically the injection of a weakened virus, a piece of a virus, or a toxin produced by a virus or bacteria into the body of an individual, sometimes coupled with an adjuvant (a substance to increase immunity response) to cause the body to produce white blood cells for the sake of fighting off infection.[27] Vaccines are not cure-alls or some nanotechnology that itself fights infection. Rather, what is injected stimulates the body's immune system so that the body can fight off future infection from related viruses and bacteria.

Because the act of vaccination involves an invasion of the body by a foreign object (a needle and solution), the Libertarian Voluntaryist principle of self-ownership comes into play. Forcing an individual to get a vaccine should be, in-and-of itself, considered an ethical harm without consent of the affected individual. Some people attempt to say that not vaccinating produces a great risk of harm to others and, thus, people who do not get vaccines are somehow endangering others and should be viewed as committing a rights violation.

This reasoning should be rejected outright when one looks at the nature of viruses and the actual actions taking place in the spread of disease. As viruses are independent agents that exist within the living cells of an organism, they should not be considered a chosen harm unless specifically procured and produced by an individual. This would be viewed no differently than someone who finds that a bee's nest has been established on a tree in their backyard or a rat's nest has been created in the roof of their home, to their annoyance. As a person is not responsible for the independent actions of other organisms, people cannot be charged with responsibility for being infected when it is not of their own will. A person should only be held accountable to the extent they create and/or privatize an independent organism such as intentionally manufacturing anthrax or purchasing a pit bull. In this framework, individuals are only responsible for their specific property rights claims taken on and are responsible for the actions that stem from that privatization.

The rightful remedy in response to risk concerns of those who are not vaccinated is to make property rules for entry to various venues. A property owner can make entry to their facilities conditioned on having certain vaccines and, within this permission, be able to bar those who have not had certain vaccines and hold responsible those who violate the rules of the property owner. This method of robustly respecting the rights of individuals and the rights of property owners is key to delineating when a harm has taken place based on specific actors and actions.

It should be noted that the fears about a lack of vaccination should be reckoned with the realities of vaccination. Vaccines are not absolute bars to illness and, as many vaccine manufacturers note, there are varying efficacy rates and protection periods depending on the specific brand and content of the vaccine. In addition, vaccines today do not protect against all possible viral and bacterial infections. Many who are eager to push vaccination onto others also do not hold themselves to a strict standard of quarantine as they return to work or school well before the infectious period abates (up to two weeks for the common cold and 8 days for the flu).

I mention these facts as a reminder that protection against spreading disease involves more than just vaccination, but a social norm of accepting that people need to be able to stay away from others for extended periods while ill so as to not spread sicknesses. This, of course, can readily be metered through a robust respect of property rights for all people.

OBJECTION 5: But what about child predation?

Child predation is a serious topic that Libertarian Voluntaryism specifically addresses. As children are self-owners under the trust relationship of a parent or other guardian, adults who attempt to perform mature acts with children, especially sexual ones, are in violation of Libertarian Voluntaryist ethics and deserve the most extreme of consequences for abusing those who cannot readily defend themselves. The question of when a child is mature enough to transition from a label of "child" to "adult" is a difficult one as it's not rooted in some arbitrary age number. Rather, it's rooted in physical and intellectual maturity and ability to be self-sufficient. Which means that, by default, any pre-pubescent child is incapable of consenting to sexual activity as they are not biologically developed for it. Those in the early years of puberty who are not living independently should also be viewed as unable to consent generally to sexual activity due to lack of maturity.

Some will try to argue nuances about whether two young teens could consent to have sex with each other. There is no special exception to the ethical principle: either a young person could consent to sex, or they could not, based on their maturity. The consequences therefrom may not be severe if the two parties are both unable to consent given their developmental independence, but to suggest that a 15-year-old can consent to sex with only a limited age bracket assumes that duress can only exist based on age. There is no logical mandate to suggest that duress automatically does or does not exist based on age. There could be just as much duress from a similarly aged teen as there could be from an adult given the context of when pressured. That said, the Libertarian Voluntaryist ethical minimum is that sexual activity is default predatory on children who are pre-pubescent. Sexual activity is best reserved for when a young person is physically mature (past early puberty) and financially independent (living on their own/able to live on their own). Unfortunately, many young people have been kept in a state of permanent infantilism thanks to public school and government market distortion keeping them from being able to become independent even into their 20s. Whatever the case, it will still be social norms and scientific development over time that helps clarify and define when a young person is able to make mature choices and have those choices respected. But that process must always be scrutinized to avoid child exploitation.

OBJECTION 6: But how can we measure consent?

The metrics for measuring consent are an evolving process based on scientific understanding and social/cultural norms. In a freed market, the metrics would naturally trend toward what most people expect to do to manifest consent and, with that, mechanisms would be developed for enhancing accuracy and minimizing duress. What this will look like is not certain until the market is freed, but we can already see many types of market solutions now, with e-signatures for contracts, arbitration and dispute resolution agencies, and other forms of confirmation such as with fingerprints and photographic verification.

A principled approach toward consent measurement is one that errs on the side of not accepting consent by default. In other words, getting consent should be something that takes effort and physical confirmation to ensure accuracy. This stringency should be higher the greater the invasiveness, intimacy, or risk involved, and dispute resolution and insurance agencies should, and likely will given existing trends, demand explicit, empirical, verifiable mechanisms for consent. Given these incentives, it is likely that market services will arise and produce means to facilitate market transactions for confirmation of consent, as exists with companies like DocuSign and PandaDoc.

OBJECTION 7: But how will people innovate without intellectual property?

One of the biggest concerns about a lack of intellectual property (IP) is that innovation will grind to a halt because people cannot be financially rewarded just for coming up with an invention alone. While at first glance this may seem reasonable as there are many inventions with serious research and development costs, the actuality of what happens is just a shift in how people get value from innovation. Some of the most obvious examples of this shift came with the advent of torrenting sites like Napster and Limewire.

With those sites, artists suddenly could not rely on the sale of physical media alone anymore because anyone around the world could download their songs without payment. This disruption was fought hard at first in the courts, but, eventually, artists had to succumb to the fact that it was all too easy to rip and distribute songs. To adapt, artists started changing how they made their money. They started offering specialized merchandise only available at live shows. They started having paid VIP meetups. They started hosting luxury performances for private parties.[28]

With the shift in digital technology, indie artists suddenly realized that they could use the framework of easily distributable music to build their fame. Instead of fighting the copying, they adapted by promoting it to gain popularity. Many bands got their start doing this on Myspace.com, releasing their tracks for free on the platform to boost fandom and create an audience they could sell live shows to.[29] The proximate property rights established on online platforms through having limited, official channels, was enough for indie artists to maintain their brand identity while monetizing through scarce, physical shows.

Later, artists adapted even further by using direct-funding models through Patreon.com, Kickstarter.com, and Indiegogo.com, to offer fans a way to support their work directly while getting special perks.[30] The direct funding method has become a wild success, with top earners like Tim Dillion making over $2 million each year from Patreon alone.[31]

Making a physical product for mass production is not quite the same as being an artist. However, that sector also had to adapt thanks to the ease of copying in China. Inventors face the difficulty that anything made over in the U.S. can readily be knocked off in China with its thousands of factories and loose enforcement on copycats.[32] To deal with this, inventors have switched to a model of focusing on customer service. Making a great product offering with support that treats customers well has become the forefront sustainable business practice. This is how American companies and inventors have still managed to compete with Chinese competitors despite the ease with which others can rip products.[33]

The switch to an open-source innovation model has its own benefits too. When innovation is open-sourced, everyone can also learn from each other. Which means that advancement in technology becomes a mutually beneficial endeavor and the monetization switches to scarce product offerings and customer service instead of holding IP. This has been especially visible in the software development market where giant corporations like Microsoft have switched gears toward working on open-source solutions so that they can benefit from the global software engineering community while focusing their sales on scarce physical resources like offering cloud services and hosting.[34]

For all the concerns about inventors not being able to be rewarded, an important reminder is that the government-crafted solution is itself arbitrary, capricious, and thieving. An inventor has 20 years for a utility patent before it expires, but few complain about the lack of inventions for products which need more than 20 years to recoup.[35] The fact that there is some arbitrary period of 20 years is enough for people to dismiss the reality that some important inventions may not come to bear, by their own logic, if the patent period is too short to recoup expenses. Additionally, the government also takes inventions by force under 35 U.S.C. 181.[36] Few people know that the Patent Office is actually a government clearinghouse made to capture inventions that would accelerate innovation too fast for state control. Patent office staff submit applications to higher-ups when they think the invention might be too dangerous to be let out for "national security." If the government claims the invention is of national security interest, the inventor is gagged (legally bound to remain silent about the invention) and is then deprived of the invention and the monetization therefrom until the invention is declassified by the state. The inventor is not entitled to any compensation from the government for their losses in R&D.

But wait, there's more! If you're an inventor and you don't want to license your invention, too bad! The government ALSO has a compulsory licensing scheme whereby others can force the inventor to license certain creative works under certain conditions.[37] So don't think that intellectual property is something magically "effective" and "just" under the government. It's not. And, often, the government legal arm is used to silence human progress and defeat innovation with patent trolls who file patents solely for the purpose of trying to sue others instead of making the product themselves.[38]

Only a free market in innovation can produce ethical outcomes and incentivize people to monetize via providing direct physical value and strong customer service.

OBJECTION 8: You just want corporations to rule!

Some try to claim that Libertarian Voluntaryists just want corporations to rule because we are against taxation as a funding mechanism. This could not be further from the truth. It is important to recognize that corporations are legal fictions chartered under the rules of government and are given immunity by the government in government courts. So, corporations, as they are, are products of state control due to the legal backdrop of government sanction and regulation through the Securities and Exchange Commission and state licensing boards.[39] Corporate businesses in the free market are just groups of people working under a common mission. A company could require that certain legal immunity is granted before doing business via individual contract, much like Sam's Club has a membership agreement with terms for customers, but this does not in itself mean that a corporation is "ruling."

For corporations to "rule," they would have to act like a state and, instead of transacting based on voluntary trade, they would be forcing their products onto people whether they wanted them or not. This would, in turn, make corporations mafias or state-like by converting voluntary business to threats and force. The concern of "corporations ruling" is no different in empirical question than the fear of having government tyranny as the government is also a corporate body of people claiming to provide a service through forcible rule. Libertarian Voluntaryists stand against ALL rulers, in any name, as rulers are those who claim to have an inherent right to your body and property by your birth.

OBJECTION 9: But how will policing be effective?

One of the psychological distortions of state action is causing people to think that "policing" and "security" are the same thing. In the world today, private security outnumbers police in most countries.[40] In addition to private security being widespread for businesses, people have their own private security patrols, security cameras, alarm systems, guard dogs, neighborhood watches, and guns to defend themselves. The private production of defense is already a market norm and, as private market security and self-defense becomes more normalized with a transition away from state control, those mechanisms will be the greatest deterrent to violent crime. In an ideal transition, police will only be relied on for apprehending criminals who violate the body or property of others for the purpose of bringing them before a court. Police will not be relied on for patrol, that is, watching and spying on people, as other market means become more robust and effective at deterring and stopping criminals in the act. For more on the economics of this process, I recommend reading *The Private Production of Defense* by Hans Hermann-Hoppe[41] and the last chapter of this book.

OBJECTION 10: But how will money work without the state?

Money is the expectation of future subjective value creation. In other words, it represents what people think they will be able to gain from others in trade. Money pre-existed the government and arose naturally from people trading in the market.[42] It started in some places with shells, in others, with rocks, and still others, with eggs. Eventually, gold and silver became the most traded mediums of exchange due to their durability, malleability, scarcity, and utility. In a freed market, people will choose a medium of exchange that works best for them based on an organic development. As facilitating trade is a global market demand, market-based money is a natural outcome of trade. The desire for sound money, also being a market demand, will lead to business practices for verification of authenticity. For more on the economic theory of money and credit, read: *The Theory of Money and Credit* by Ludwig von Mises.

OBJECTION 11: What if someone is drunk? Can they consent?

Each person is responsible for their own choices. To the extent that someone makes a poor choice while under the influence of a substance, they should be held liable by default except when their inebriation was forced upon them, for example, when someone is slipped a drug. This default responsibility helps to ensure that each person only alters their consciousness in a safe manner. Market norms may end up forgiving or lessening consequences or alleviating duties due to a lack of sobriety, but this should not be the default norm to avoid people trying to escape responsibility for their actions.

OBJECTION 12: What about imposters?

Fraud is a contractual harm where one person is making a material misrepresentation of fact about a trade with another to induce the deal. If someone tries to impersonate another, or another's business, it would be a property rights violation if an exchange took place on that misrepresentation. In a Libertarian Voluntaryist justice system, those who pretend to be another person or another business to trick someone into doing business with them should be held liable for their fraud at the point the transaction takes place.

OBJECTION 13: What if someone revokes their consent?

Consent can always be revoked in line with respecting the sovereign property right of the individual. However, if someone revokes consent and they otherwise entered into a contractual agreement, they can be held liable according to the terms of their agreement. Market norms in dispute resolution will come into play in deciding the consequences of revocation when other duties exist.

In the event someone revokes consent to a property right where initial consent was given, such as a pilot revoking mid-flight the consent given for a passenger to fly on a commercial airplane, the consent offeror cannot escalate harms in removing the person whose consent to being present is revoked. The pilot of the craft would be committing an escalation of force by trying to kick the passenger out of the plane from the sky mid-flight.

This thinking is in line with the Libertarian Voluntaryist ethic of attempting to minimize the initiation of force as among humans. If a passenger is unruly, they may be restrained until landing and then safely removed. If a passenger escalates force, force may be escalated against them accordingly to restrain or incapacitate them in defense of others.

OBJECTION 14: But what about self-defense situations?

The chief Libertarian Voluntaryist solution to unwanted intrusions is a right of removal, which is a right to physically remove trespassers or remove unwanted intrusions of physical touch. Escalation of force should be avoided as best as possible in doing so, meaning, removal should be performed only as needed to get the person off the subject property. To the extent a trespasser resists, it is justified for the property owner to use adequate force to overcome the resistance and successfully remove the trespasser.

Deadly use of force in self-defense is reserved for situations where someone is either making an imminent threat of impending deadly force or is using actual deadly force. What makes a threat imminent depends on the actions and capacities of the person making the threat, and such situations will ultimately be judged in a court or other dispute resolution arbitration based on consensual market choices.

When it comes to defense of the home, deadly force is acceptable as a default norm to those breaking and entering because the home is the sanctuary of the individual. The home is constructed precisely for the protection of life against all threats outside, thus, a person breaking and entering into another's home by force is making the manifest threat against the sanctuary protecting the life of those living inside.

To the extent that anyone is in a place they have an ethical right to be, there is never a duty to retreat from attackers. Every person is justified in defending their body against physical attacks from others when attacked or when another threatens an attack and moves toward making an attack.

By the Libertarian Voluntaryist principle of estoppel, anyone who initiates force against others cannot ethically claim that the same cannot be done to them. Which means that, at a bare minimum, a person who strikes another cannot claim that they should not be hit back in-kind. But again, reducing escalation is key to helping reduce conflict as among humans with the Libertarian Voluntaryist principles in mind.

10

NOW HOW DO WE GET THERE?

Now that you have a good sense about what it means to hold a Libertarian Voluntaryist philosophy, the big question remains: How do we get there in practice? How do we get to a point where the culture around the world starts to shift to one where people value respecting each other's consent, their bodies, and their physical property?

The change first starts with you.

Work on yourself and your self-knowledge. Think deeply about the ways you have been affected by others and the influences that have rationalized violent state force, from what was taught in public school, to what you've seen on T.V. Much of what people do when confronted with challenges to their statist worldview is REACTION because they've been brainwashed by authoritarians in school and in the media to love central planning and to fear anything that challenges the omnipotent state.

A big part of escaping the indoctrination of statism is letting go of the things you cannot control. At this point in time, unless you're a president, governor, or sheriff, there is likely little you can do directly on your own to make big changes with state action. What you CAN DO is talk to those you're closest with about these ideas. Your friends. Your family. People you discuss ideas with on social media. Talking about these principles with others is a great way to challenge yourself and think about the common excuses people make for unethical action. And, it will help refine your articulations in the process.

To get ready for those next steps, I highly recommend you read the following two books:

Healing The Child Within: Discovery and Recovery for Adult Children of Dysfunctional Families Paperback by Charles L. Whitfield M.D.

Nonviolent Communication: A Language of Life, 3rd Edition: Life-Changing Tools for Healthy Relationships by Marshall B. Rosenberg Ph.D.

These books above will help you heal from past trauma and guide you to be a better communicator as you explore Libertarian Voluntaryist philosophy.

THE POLITICAL ADVOCACY FOR THOSE ON THE FENCE

While talking philosophy and psychology is wonderful, many people are afraid to leave their statist baggage behind unless they have a specific vision to transition to. The good news is that there has never been a better time to dive into the liberty sphere with all the growth in the past 20 years. The principles of liberty have taken root in the alt media space. Scholarship at Mises.org and LewRockwell.com provide great resources on philosophy and economics, and liberty-oriented thinktanks like The Independent Institute and the Foundation for Economic Education help report on Libertarian Voluntaryist pursuits in our current time. Libertarian Voluntaryist philosophy has even been mentioned on shows like Joe Rogan, Tim Pool, and Dave Rubin, and on many other alternative networks reaching millions of people.

The most common call-to-action in the movement is getting government out of our lives and wallets. However, the means to that end differ across a spectrum. Some advocate for government policy change via political means with the Libertarian Party. Some advocate for state nullification and secession. Others wish to build new living environments like with the Seasteading Institute and their mission to create experimental islands. And then, there are some people calling themselves Agorists who think the black market, that is, market dealings performed outside state approval, will eventually overshadow the government's control.

These tactics and theories all have their various merits, but few can articulate a practical advocacy which can shift the government expediently into a fully voluntary society while easing the common concerns of those worried about political stability in transition. To fill the gap, I would ask for the Libertarian Voluntaryist movement to get behind the "not-for-profit" government model as a transitioning argument.

What does that mean? Well, it means that, like any not-for-profit corporation, the governments of the world will no longer maintain a monopoly on anything but, will instead, compete with the private market for revenue and services. To stay afloat, the U.S. government will have to rely on voluntary contributions from individuals who will have the ability to make specific or general gifts to the government. The underlying principle is this: When the government no longer can collect money with the threat of force, only that which people truly value will be funded.

So, for example, if people no longer want a massive Department of Defense bombing every country possible, people will simply no longer fund the military and will drain it of its resources. Likewise, if the people are tired of the BATF or the Department of Education, people can choose to specify where their money will go, if at all.

The benefits are numerous:

-    The government can no longer ignore the financial will of people.

-    Programs which receive little support will go defunct by virtue of not being funded.

-    Private alternatives will be given the chance to arise. (Such as private education, postage, security, etc.)

-    The government will be unable to do more than what people are voluntarily funding it for.

The best way to initially effect this policy is to allow earmarks to specific departments. How the departments carry out their function should be left to policy initiatives because earmarks per issue will be very burdensome to carry out (just imagine if the government accepted funds for courts but the donor exempts "rape" cases – very tough to manage the request and even tougher not to intermingle funds). Also, funding by department will swiftly reveal what programs people find most/least valuable.

Moving toward a "not-for-profit" form of government shouldn't be the end of the story. The people of America and others around the world ought to advocate for government downsizing in other ways such as with decriminalization, overseas troop withdrawal, and auction.

But I believe that no single act (short of ending the Federal Reserve) could be more profound at reshaping the political sphere for liberty. Everything the government does will hinge on its ability to pay. When the public can cut the government off like any other product, the people gain significant control over their lives. This turning of government into a not-for-profit could be likened to the Articles of Confederation, but it should go beyond the Federal government to include states, counties, cities, and other subdivisions. When the government is totally dependent on the voluntary support of people's wallets, then it will finally have to meet their demands or face radical losses.

COMPARING CURRENT NOT-FOR-PROFIT PHILOSOPHY TO THE GOVERNMENT NOT-FOR-PROFIT

The reason the not-for-profit model is so attractive is that it forces the government to engage the people if it wants money. Much like any other good or service provider in the free market, the government will have to prove its worth to receive benefits. This requires a two-way relationship that truly looks to the values of the constituents instead of relying on coercive force to pilfer wealth. It also promotes transparency, as any attempts to hide what is going on will further skepticism followed by detraction. Just like any other not-for-profit, if the government cannot demonstrate what it is doing with your money, you and the other supporters will be reluctant to give. If the government is not perceived as producing efficient value, then people are all the more likely to turn to the free market for a solution.

Some may argue that this will cause a collective action problem where the rich/business owners end up paying more because the poor won't pay anything. This may be true, but that is already happening in the current market. As it stands, most taxes already come from the rich and business owners.[43] The largest corporations and associations are also those who have the resources to spend significantly on lobbying.[44]

This being the case, the business class of America has an incentive to bear the burden if they find that the American governmental system provides them value. For example, if business owners think the local courthouses and police are doing a great job at stopping theft and vandalism, they will be incentivized to continue to donate. In a sense, it could be a point of pride for businesses to advertise their contribution to the government. Just like Walmart has poster boards showing who they support in the community, a business may advertise their support of certain things like the police, courthouses, and national defense, to tell the community they care. It sounds superficial, but that's already our state of public relations and marketing.[45]

As for outcome, if there is underfunding, and that causes a material harm to the public through increased crime/violence, then it is logical that businesses and individuals will give more money to the government if they think it is worth it. Or, possibly, they will find a better method in the market if that is attractive.

This concept already comports with the current model of government. No place is crime-free, and, when crime increases or other social problems arise, members of the legislature craft legislation and present it to the public to address the issues. Why couldn't this same process be done at the local level, including not just policy but the strings to the purse itself?

To summarize other concerns, the not-for-profit model of government shares no different critique than that of the theft-funded (tax-funded) government. Fear of government bribery? Already exists.[46] Fear of new criminal riots? Already exists.[47] Fear of nuclear threats? Already exists.[48] Fear of money going missing? The Pentagon has that to the tune of trillions.[49]

The changes people will find between the not-for-profit and the tax-funded government is that they will save money on tax compliance (because it doesn't exist), save money on wasteful government spending, and save their psyche from the constant threat of force against people and their property.

FURTHER MECHANISMS OF FUNDING

In addition to voluntary donation, the government could also raise funds via voluntary means through offerings like lotteries and paid trainings. For a comparative to what exists now, the Florida Lottery raised $2.2 billion for the Educational Enhancement Trust Fund in 2020 alone.[50] Now, imagine what it would look like if the various governments ran lotteries based on specific needs, like they had a "Roads Lottery" or a "Fire Department Scratch-Off." Given that it's already a successful tactic, it's not hard to imagine what could be accomplished if this was promoted to fund the government without the coercion and threats of jail.

On top of funding mechanisms like lotteries, the government could change how national defense is funded in defense against other governments. Instead of trainees being paid, the government could offer certificate courses where people pay to get training. Depending on what makes sense with the experience of those running the trainings, candidates could be required to accumulate a certain number of training certificates before being considered for acceptance to a basic training position to participate as a soldier in the making. Soldiers could then be funded by a mix of monies raised from the trainings and by voluntary support, much like Christian missionaries are supported in Campus Crusade for Christ where volunteers do their own fundraising for their ministry roles. In operating this way, a unified national defense in transition becomes a voluntary service funded only by willing participants, ending the perverse incentive of joining for the sake of getting a paycheck and/or college tuition in exchange for following orders.

RESTITUTION AND DISMANTLING

To further divest resources from the state to the private sector while also providing restitution to harmed parties, the government could sell off land and resources at auctions over a course of years. Imagine that the government starts by selling off buildings and land of agencies that would be defunct under Libertarian Voluntaryist norms, like the DEA and ATF. The government could accept payment at the auctions in dollars and then, with the proceeds, remit the money to the public at large in dollars much like people got checks in 2020 under the CARES ACT.

Naturally, companies would vie to get their hands on the dollars so they could use the money at auction, incentivizing trade for goods and services in dollars. In this manner, the government could divest holdings over time while giving people a form of refund in the process.

While it may not perfectly restitute, it would at least end the conflict over scarce resources through privatization, signal who values the resources most through auction, and offer an opportunity for people to get something out of their past stolen resources.

For restitution of those specially harmed by the state, such as those put into prison for victimless crimes, those who lost their home to eminent domain, or those otherwise stolen from over a victimless crime, the government could offer restitution in land tracts from the existing Federal holdings. Again, while not perfect restitution, it's a means to restitution without creating more conflict over scarce resources via shared ownership and it divests the government of holdings with a move toward privatization.

All accounting for these transactions would be made public for confirmation via a Web portal and, given that the auctions are public, everyone would be able to see exactly how the cash is flowing. A portion of the proceeds could be used to fund the auction management and disposition, something under 10 percent of gross. The result would be that, after a period of auctions taking place over 10 years or so, the Federal government would be divested of most all major holdings save what might be left in the most critical elements of mutually-assured-destruction (M.A.D.) defenses against foreign governments, such as maintaining the nuclear silos and the space missile defense systems.

So please, take time to think through this model as a reasonable means by which we can transition away from the violent force of the state. Use this framing to convince others that there is a practical, intelligent method for moving government toward a voluntary society without facing a total collapse or vulnerability to other government invasion.

The "not-for-profit" government model is not the total solution, or end, but what other policy can transform the government toward Libertarian Voluntaryism while still maintaining relative stability?

If you can think of it, I would love to hear it.

ABOUT THE AUTHOR

Jack Lloyd is a Libertarian Voluntaryist who has been promoting a principled message of liberty for over 15 years. He holds a Bachelor of Science in Public Relations, business concentration, and a Juris Doctor. He's worked as a juvenile defense attorney and, later, as a government school teacher. He left the schooling paradigm to open his own tutoring company after seeing how much children were hurt by the schooling process. His experiences working with kids as a lawyer and teacher also led him to help families exit compulsory schooling through his page, The Honest Teacher. These days, he keeps occupied as a producer, making music, comic books, educational videos, and memes for a variety of outlets from The Pholosopher to Voluntaryist – The Comic Series.

You can connect with him over at:

www.volcomic.com

&

www.thepholosopher.com

REFERENCES

1 "Brain Basics: Know Your Brain." National Institute of Neurological Disorders and Stroke, U.S. Department of Health and Human Services, https://www.ninds.nih.gov/Disorders/Patient-Caregiver-Education/Know-Your-Brain.

2 Kinsella, Stephan. "Against Intellectual Property: Stephan Kinsella." Mises Institute, 18 Aug. 2014, https://mises.org/library/against-intellectual-property-0.

3 "Sumer." Wikipedia, Wikimedia Foundation, 14 Jan. 2022, https://en.wikipedia.org/wiki/Sumer.

4 "Government of the United Kingdom." Wikipedia, Wikimedia Foundation, 12 Jan. 2022, https://en.wikipedia.org/wiki/Government_of_the_United_Kingdom.

5 History of Voting in America - Washington Secretary of State. https://www.sos.wa.gov/_assets/elections/history-of-voting-in-america-timeline.pdf.

6 Chandler, Nathan. "Who Was the World's First King?" HowStuffWorks Science, HowStuffWorks, 17 Dec. 2020, https://science.howstuffworks.com/environmental/earth/archaeology/first-king.htm.

7 "Divine Right of Kings." Wikipedia, Wikimedia Foundation, 1 Jan. 2022, https://en.wikipedia.org/wiki/Divine_right_of_kings.

8 "No Treason. No. Vi. The Constitution of No Authority (1870)." Online Library of Liberty, https://oll.libertyfund.org/title/spooner-no-treason-no-vi-the-constitution-of-no-authority-1870.

9 O'Sullivan, Andrea, et al. "How the FAA Killed Uber for Planes." *Reason.com*, 27 June 2017, https://reason.com/2017/06/27/how-the-faa-killed-uber-for-planes/.

10 Hazlett, Thomas W., et al. "We Could Have Had Cellphones Four Decades Earlier." Reason.com, 11 June 2017, https://reason.com/2017/06/11/we-could-have-had-cellphones-f/.

11 Swain, J E, et al. "Approaching the Biology of Human Parental Attachment: Brain Imaging, Oxytocin and Coordinated Assessments of Mothers and Fathers." Brain Research, U.S. National Library of Medicine, 11 Sept. 2014, https://www.ncbi.nlm.nih.gov/pmc/articles/PMC4157077/.

12 Johnson, Sara B, et al. "Adolescent Maturity and the Brain: The Promise and Pitfalls of Neuroscience Research in Adolescent Health Policy." The Journal of Adolescent Health : Official Publication of the Society for Adolescent Medicine, U.S. National Library of Medicine, Sept. 2009, https://www.ncbi.nlm.nih.gov/pmc/articles/PMC2892678/.

13 Against School - John Taylor Gatto, https://www.wesjones.com/gatto1.htm.

14 Fox, Carolyn Shepard. "Home." Home | Sudbury Valley School, https://sudburyvalley.org/.

15 "Miscarriage." Wikipedia, Wikimedia Foundation, 9 Jan. 2022, https://en.wikipedia.org/wiki/Miscarriage.

16 "Evictionism." Wikipedia, Wikimedia Foundation, 30 Nov. 2021, https://en.wikipedia.org/wiki/Evictionism#:~:text=Eviction ism%20is%20a%20moral%20theory,abortion%20based%2 0on%20property%20rights.

17 Reitz, Kevin. "How and Why Is the American Punishment System 'Exceptional'?" Criminal Law, 23 Apr. 2018, https://crim.jotwell.com/how-and-why-is-the-american-punishment-system-exceptional/.

18 "The Psychological Impact of Incarceration: Implications for Post-Prison Adjustment." ASPE, https://aspe.hhs.gov/reports/psychological-impact-incarceration-implications-post-prison-adjustment-0.

19 Williams, Adrian C, and Lisa J Hill. "Meat and Nicotinamide: A Causal Role in Human Evolution, History, and Demographics." International Journal of Tryptophan Research : IJTR, SAGE Publications, 2 May 2017, https://www.ncbi.nlm.nih.gov/pmc/articles/PMC5417583/.

20 Shah, Sabir. "The US Has Been at War 225 out of 243 Years since 1776." Thenews, The News International, 9 Jan. 2020, https://www.thenews.com.pk/print/595752-the-us-has-been-at-war-225-out-of-243-years-since-1776.

21 20th Century Democide, https://www.hawaii.edu/powerkills/20TH.HTM.

22 Nazaryan, Alexander. "The US Department of Defense Is One of the World's Biggest Polluters." Newsweek, 23 Feb. 2016, https://www.newsweek.com/2014/07/25/us-department-defence-one-worlds-biggest-polluters-259456.html.

23 "U.S. and Five Gulf States Reach Historic Settlement with BP to Resolve Civil Lawsuit over Deepwater Horizon Oil Spill." The United States Department of Justice, 14 Nov. 2016, https://www.justice.gov/opa/pr/us-and-five-gulf-states-reach-historic-settlement-bp-resolve-civil-lawsuit-over-deepwater.

24 Chappell, Bill. "EPA Says It Released 3 Million Gallons of Contaminated Water into River." NPR, NPR, 10 Aug. 2015, https://www.npr.org/sections/thetwo-way/2015/08/10/431223703/epa-says-it-released-3-million-gallons-of-contaminated-water-into-river.

25 "Pollution in China." Wikipedia, Wikimedia Foundation, 4 Jan. 2022, https://en.wikipedia.org/wiki/Pollution_in_China.

26 "About • the Ocean Cleanup." The Ocean Cleanup, 18 Nov. 2021, https://theoceancleanup.com/about/.

27 The Children's Hospital of Philadelphia. "Developments by Year." Children's Hospital of Philadelphia, The Children's Hospital of Philadelphia, 20 Nov. 2014, https://www.chop.edu/centers-programs/vaccine-education-center/vaccine-history/developments-by-year.

28 Gamal, Ashraf El. The Evolution of the Music Industry in the Post-Internet Era. https://scholarship.claremont.edu/cgi/viewcontent.cgi?article=1501&context=cmc_theses.

29 Katyirizarry. "16 Bands Who Got Their Start on Myspace." Loudwire, 20 June 2019, https://loudwire.com/bands-who-got-start-on-myspace/.

30 Robertson, Adi. "Inside Patreon, the Economic Engine of Internet Culture." The Verge, The Verge, 3 Aug. 2017, https://www.theverge.com/2017/8/3/16084248/patreon-profile-jack-conte-crowdfunding-art-politics-culture.

31 "The Tim Dillon Show Is Creating a Podcast." Patreon, https://www.patreon.com/thetimdillonshow.

32 "How to Get Something Made in China in 2019 (Step by Step!): Location Rebel." YouTube, 13 Feb. 2019, https://youtu.be/2dY0-N2L8So.

33 Xin Wang and Z. Justin Ren. "How to Compete in China's e-Commerce Market." MIT Sloan Management Review, 18 Sept. 2012, https://sloanreview.mit.edu/article/how-to-compete-in-chinas-e-commerce-market/.

34 Warren, Tom. "Microsoft: We Were Wrong about Open Source." The Verge, The Verge, 18 May 2020, https://www.theverge.com/2020/5/18/21262103/microsoft-open-source-linux-history-wrong-statement.

35 "How Long Does Patent, Trademark or Copyright Protection Last?How Long Do IPR Rights Last?" How Long Does Patent, Trademark or Copyright Protection Last? | STOPfakes.gov - Intellectual Property Rights Resources and Assistance, https://www.stopfakes.gov/article?id=How-Long-Does-Patent-Trademark-or-Copyright-Protection-Last.

36 G.W. Schulz, Center for Investigative Reporting. "Government Secrecy Orders on Patents Have Stifled More than 5,000 Inventions." Wired, Conde Nast, 16 Apr. 2013, https://www.wired.com/2013/04/gov-secrecy-orders-on-patents/.

37 "Compulsory License." Wikipedia, Wikimedia Foundation, 7 Dec. 2021, https://en.wikipedia.org/wiki/Compulsory_license.

38 "Patent Troll." Wikipedia, Wikimedia Foundation, 16 Jan. 2022, https://en.wikipedia.org/wiki/Patent_troll.

39 "United States Corporate Law." Wikipedia, Wikimedia Foundation, 22 Dec. 2021, https://en.wikipedia.org/wiki/United_States_corporate_law.

40 McCarthy, Niall. "Private Security Outnumbers the Police in Most Countries Worldwide [Infographic]." Forbes, Forbes Magazine, 31 Aug. 2017, https://www.forbes.com/sites/niallmccarthy/2017/08/31/private-security-outnumbers-the-police-in-most-countries-worldwide-infographic/?sh=47f59f96210f.

41 Hans-Hermann, Hoppe. "The Private Production of Defense: Hans-Hermann Hoppe." Mises Institute, 18 Aug. 2014, https://mises.org/library/private-production-defense.

42 "What Is Money?" The Pholosopher, 23 Sept. 2019, https://youtu.be/BFmQv728Q0I.

43 York, Erica. "Summary of the Latest Federal Income Tax Data, 2021 Update." Tax Foundation, 18 Jan. 2022, https://taxfoundation.org/federal-income-tax-data-2021/.

44 "Top Lobbying Firms." OpenSecrets, https://www.opensecrets.org/federal-lobbying/top-lobbying-firms?cycle=2021.

45 "Corporate Social Responsibility." Wikipedia, Wikimedia Foundation, 12 Jan. 2022, https://en.wikipedia.org/wiki/Corporate_social_responsibility.

46 "US State Department Official Charged with Accepting Bribes from Chinese Spies." The Guardian, Guardian News and Media, 29 Mar. 2017, https://www.theguardian.com/world/2017/mar/29/us-state-department-bribes-china-spies-candace-claiborne.

47 "2020–2022 United States Racial Unrest." Wikipedia, Wikimedia Foundation, 18 Jan. 2022, https://en.wikipedia.org/wiki/2020%E2%80%932022_United_States_racial_unrest.

48 "North Korea and Weapons of Mass Destruction."
Wikipedia, Wikimedia Foundation, 10 Jan. 2022,
https://en.wikipedia.org/wiki/North_Korea_and_weapons_o
f_mass_destruction.

49 "The Pentagon's $35 Trillion Accounting Black Hole."
Yahoo!, Yahoo!, https://www.yahoo.com/now/pentagon-35-
trillion-accounting-black-231154593.html.

50 "About." Capital Soup, 2 Aug. 2021,
https://capitalsoup.com/2021/08/02/florida-lottery-
celebrates-end-of-fiscal-year-with-record-sales-and-
education-contributions/.

Made in the USA
Columbia, SC
12 May 2023

16531048R00054